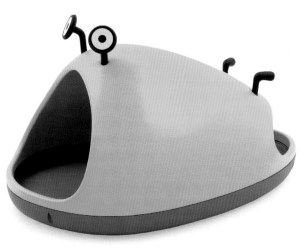

Designed for Kids
Phyllis Richardson

A complete sourcebook

With 754 color illustrations

Thames & Hudson

Designed for Kids
Contents

Designed for Kids
Introduction

Let us now praise inventors of children's products. While this book has a
lot of high design, a lot of eye-catching masterpieces that will send people
reaching for their wallets, there is also a lot of design that just makes the
day-to-day work of carrying, walking, changing, even appeasing, small children
a little less trying, and much more aesthetically pleasing. Some of these are
simply brilliant new designs that follow logical systems of functionality and
meet today's stringent safety standards. Most are also beautiful to look at
and touch, roll, stroke, sit on or use. And, because of the development of
many of these designs has raced ahead only in the last decade or so, they
herald a new century's approach to childrearing. While there are classic
children's products that will never fade from their iconic status in the
design-conscious playroom, there is a wave of newcomers that promises, if
not to eclipse the best that has been, certainly to generate equal excitement
about what is now available and yet to come.

The current design boom certainly does not mark the first time over
the last century that children's products have been improved upon by skilled,
qualified designers. Gerrit Rietveld created a range in the 1920s for his own
children that included the wooden 'beach buggy' with coloured squares in
his iconic patterning. Charles Eames and Verner Panton, whose products
are both featured in these pages, both created scaled-down versions of some
of their furnishings so that children could be included in the larger design
scheme. It says something about the current climate in children's design that
Panton's idea for a child-sized version of his moulded-plastic chair was
developed in the 1960s, but has only recently been found financially viable
to produce in quantity. Enzo Mari's wooden puzzle 'Animali', which marked
the beginning of his association with the Italian firm Danese in 1957, has
become a design classic and is now available as a limited edition.

But the movement today is of a greater magnitude than these separate
design achievements, involving the spectrum of designers from large
manufacturers to individuals based in garage-workshops. One sign that
something special was happening in the world of children's design appeared
in 2003, when design giant Offi launched their children's range with a
stable of world-class designers, including Eric Pfeiffer, Karim Rashid and
Roberto Gil. Italian design group Magis came out with its Metoo collection

in 2005, featuring pieces by Finnish legend Eero Aarnio, as well as Marcel Wanders, Javier Mariscal and Enzo Mari, whose 'rational design' has come back into favour. In 2007 came a range by UK home-design store Habitat of children's products created by or with a cohort of celebrity personalities.

Most of the products presented here have been created since 2000, and, of the individual inventors, most are parents themselves who, faced with inadequate designs for pushchairs, strollers, highchairs, cots or toys, decided to make those objects or devices that they and their children craved. As far as market research is concerned, parent inventors have ideal resources playing at their feet, even if those same resources make it difficult to have lengthy periods of creative productivity. In other cases products are coming from established manufacturers who are catching on to the market for better-designed products and higher expectations they have created. Still other designs are produced by collaborative workshops and are born of extensive research into children's development and learning. The results can be as simple as a child's step stool or as complex as the many patented features of a quarto-suspension buggy that can transform to four different modes of use, includes advanced brake assemblages, safety harness, telescoping handles and pneumatic tyres.

Given that raising small children makes as many physical demands as it does mental and emotional, the devices that ease the exhausting load of childrearing are welcome in all quarters. A pushchair, for example, that can be steered with one hand is of enormous relief, as is a highchair that has more than one height setting. But then there is a very different, but equally satisfying, feeling of wrapping a baby in a blanket made of natural fibres woven to unearthly softness. If it also has a subtly sophisticated and wonderfully appealing motif then it becomes an aesthetic object as well, as does the racing car in highly lacquered solid wood. No one is saying that children should be raised to worship high design, but if the act of caring for them can be raised up so that the fine feelings are given expression in fine fabrics or a well-turned handle, and we might make ourselves happier parents being able to hold or turn it, then design has fulfilled functions beyond expectations. And as parents, we can only applaud that achievement.

Mobility

**Car Seats, Pushchairs/Strollers
Buggy Attachments & Bike Trailers**

The first baby buggy is thought to have been designed in England in 1739 by William Kent for the 3rd Duke of Devonshire. Looking like a miniature horse-drawn carriage, it was pulled by a small animal, such as a goat. With wooden wheels, it probably rolled along well, but like its immediate followers, including those used by Queen Victoria, it was not very safe. The Silver Cross perambulator, later known as the 'Rolls Royce' of baby buggies, was introduced in 1877. It was much safer and better equipped for a baby, but still a luxury item.

In the 20th century the buggy or pushchair became an essential piece of kit for most families. In 1965 MacLaren helped make using public transport a lot easier with the invention of the collapsible or 'umbrella' stroller. For urban dwellers, the buggy or pram is as much a daily necessity as the family car, and in recent years their design has had an overhaul. Car seats, too, have evolved so that parents no longer have to unwrap and disentangle a sleeping baby to transfer from one mode of transport to the next. Today, mobility is all about flexibility. Integrated systems cradle the baby from car to buggy to home without even having to unbuckle the seatbelts. Buggies are washable, collapsible, have rubber or pneumatic tyres, shock absorbers, screens and shades as well as complex braking systems. Large pram beds are back in style in modern materials and colours, and are now detachable, and reversible. We can now also walk, jog, run, cycle, and even ski, with our children safely tucked away in their own buggy compartment.

Euro Turn

Aprica, Italy
www.aprica-italia.it

The Aprica Euro Turn design was inspired by research that suggests
that allowing babies to lie flat enhances their breathing and circulation,
and offers better protection from stop-and-start movement in the car, in
addition to helping prevent traumatic impact during an accident. This
is not a lightweight, all-purpose carrier: the Euro Turn is especially
concerned with securing small babies (under the age of 6 months, from
2.5 kg/5½ lb). It is mounted similarly to most car seats in a forward-
or rear-facing direction, but the inner 'bed' of the seat can then be
rotated and clicked into a highly stable flattened position up to 170
degrees. Harness and additional padding around the baby's head ensure
the baby is snugly secured. Once a child is older, the seat can be used in a
more conventional position up to 4 years of age (maximum 18 kg/39 lb).
A thermal ventilation system keeps babies from overheating, and double-
layer head protection and a cushioned foot pad give added security.

iZi Sleep

HTS BeSafe, Norway
www.izisleep.com

Norwegian company HTS BeSafe, the only Scandinavian manufacturer of car seats, reportedly spent three years and around two million euros developing the iZi Sleep, which they now claim 'should be the safest on the market'. Having spent forty or so years testing car seats, they feel qualified to make the claim. Outside of the car the iZi Sleep can recline, to allow babies to lie flat, as recommended for better circulation, digestion and respiration. The ergonomically designed seat has additional side-impact protection provided through deep side wings. BeSafe argue that incorrect installation is one of the most significant problems with infant car seats, so they added a 'safe-to-drive' indicator that signals whether the seat has been secured properly. Different adaptors allow the seat to be used with a variety of pushchairs, or strollers.

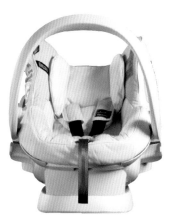

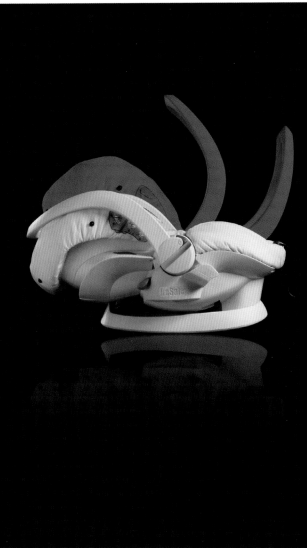

Orbit Infant Car Seat

Orbit Baby, USA
www.orbitbaby.com

Part of an integrated travel system, the Orbit Infant
Car Seat is a deep seat with ample side-impact
protection that fits via the unique Orbit SmartHub
docking system onto the Orbit Stroller chassis (see
p. 19), rocker base (see p. 19) or car-seat base. Similar
to the European ISOfix system, the Orbit Car Seat and
separate base are secured permanently in the car.
Once the base is installed, the circular hub on the seat
bottom locks into the base from any angle. The seat
can be rotated to face rearwards or forwards. The
Orbit Infant System includes car seat, base and stroller.
The infant seat fits from newborn to 10 kg (22 lb).

takata04-neo

Ichiro Iwasaki
Takata, Japan
www.iwasaki-design-studio.net

Industrial designer Ichiro Iwasaki became known for
his work on electronics such as car audio systems,
digital cameras and mobile phones. His design for
a child's safety seat maintains his minimalist modern
style while incorporating up-to-date safety features.
The designer describes its most distinctive of these as
the 'Preloader system', which helped garner a rating
as the best-performing child car seat by a Japanese
government survey. The system means that the force
used to secure it, which can be rather small, is
translated into a force of around 100 kg (220 lb) by
the seatbelt winder that wraps the belt around a
shaft that is tightened by turning a handle. Once the
maximum tension has been achieved the handle
spins easily, ensuring the seat has been properly
installed. For rear or forward-facing positions, from
newborn up to 4 years (approximately 18 kg/40 lb).

Bébé Confort Axiss

Bébé Confort/Dorel, Netherlands
www.bebeconfort.com

In a well-populated field of car seats the designers at Bébé Confort have identified a universal flaw in child car seats: the awkward job of securing children inside while bending around inside the backseat. The Axiss has standard and exceptional safety features and five reclining positions, but it is the ability to swivel 90 degrees on its base that will probably attract the most excitement. With the seat secured in its L-shaped base, it can be turned (right or left) to face the door so that the child can be set in the seat and locked in from a relatively comfortable face-on position and then turned forward for the car journey. It is designed for children from 9 months to about 4 years (9–18 kg/20–39 lb).

Maxi-Cosi CabrioFix

Maxi-Cosi/Dorel, Netherlands
www.maxi-cosi.com

Many new pushchairs, or strollers, of European design
are compatible with the Maxi-Cosi seat. This award-
winning 2006 model has greater side-impact protection
and what the makers say is 'a unique built-in seat
adjuster' that can be altered to suit a child's weight
and therefore offer better positioning and safety, as
well as a built-in seat canopy. Rear-facing only, it can
be secured in the car with a standard three-point
seatbelt or using EasyBase (secured with seatbelt
prior to installation of seat) or ISOfix base (installed
using seatbelt and adjustable support leg). It is
suitable from birth to 12–15 months (13 kg/28½ lb).

iZi Combi

HTS BeSafe, Norway
www.hts.no

The team of HTS and BeSafe have developed a range
of car seats and boosters to suit children from birth
to 12 years. The iZi Combi must surely be one of the
most well-protected seats for 0–4 years. The rear- and
forward-facing seat has a stabilizer at the rear that
anchors to the floor of the car. It also boasts 'energy-
absorbing side protection to protect the child's head,
neck and inner organs', as well as an 'anchor' at the
front of the seat to ensure the car seat belt is properly
tightened. The seat can be adjusted to five positions
for sitting or sleeping, and comes in a range of covers,
including sun canopy.

Bébé Confort
Créatis.fix

Bébé Confort/Dorel, Netherlands
www.bebeconfort.com

The latest of the popular Bébé Confort range is larger
than previous models to accommodate more room
for the baby as well as a cushioned headrest and
removable 'body support pillow', which allows baby
to lie flatter. The deeper shape, with increased side-
impact protection, and washable covers, is also a bit
longer to last a growing child. The seat works with a
separate base unit that fits in the car with a standard
three-point harness. The seat then clicks into place in
the base, making it easier to install securely. A visual
indicator confirms proper installation. It is suitable
from birth to about 12 months (13 kg/28¼ lb).

Junior HiDX

Aprica, Italy
www.aprica-italia.it

The company whose pediatric
research helped them develop
the ultra-safe, flat-lying Euro Turn
(see p. 10) have come up with a
Junior HiDX car seat with an
adjustable high seatback, wide
wings to support the neck and
posture during sleep, and a
removable 'impact shield' to help
protect the child's chest and
abdomen in the event of an
accident. A ventilated seat cushion
helps reduce heat and moisture.
The car seat is suitable from 9
months to 36 kg/83 lb.

Maxi-Cosi
Rodi XR

Maxi-Cosi/Dorel, Canada
www.maxi-cosi.com

This is an upgrade of the
company's Rodi XP and gives
a whole new sense of style to
travelling in the back seat. It has
an enhanced side protection
system and can be reclined using
an 'easy-to-reach, front-mounted
recline handle' even when a child
is already sleeping. Top-tether
device anchors the seat to the
head-rest. Available in a range of
colourways, the seat is installed
using the EasyBase (see p. 14).

Traveller

Mutsy B.V., Netherlands
www.mutsy.com

Cees Driessen established the Mutsaerts brand in 1937; his son Freek Driessen started his own company, Mutsy, in 1994 and took over Mutsaerts after his father retired in the late 1990s. The brand created a new wide range of products in 2007, the first for over five years, including a variety of compatible designs, from strollers and pushchairs to car seats and high chairs. All adhere to a design ethos of simplicity and modernity set off with vibrant colours. The Traveller is suitable from birth to 9 months (10 kg/22 lb in car, 13 kg/28 lb on stroller frame) and is available in eighteen colours. The model features an aluminium handle that can be both laid flat and used in multiple positions, including horizontal, which is healthier for babies over longer periods. It includes a removable seat and increaser for smaller babies. Traveller adapts to all Mutsy pushchairs, or strollers except the Slider (see pp. 24–5).

Soho All-Terrain Stroller

bloom, Hong Kong, USA, Europe
www.bloombaby.com

According to their mission statement, bloom was founded by 'four dads wanting to bring meaningful innovation and contemporary design to a range of baby products'. With the 'four dads', Francisco Balderrama (USA), Jason Lewis (Europe/Asia), Jon Lake (Hong Kong), and Simon May (USA/Asia) settled in so many countries, bloom is a small but truly internationally based company. The products are designed in Europe under the direction of Jon Lake (formerly of Frog Design). The Soho pushchair, or stroller, has a distinctive shape and style and high-function features such as an easy fold mechanism, lightweight alloy construction and infinity™ lie-flat seat that converts from newborn bassinet to seating position, and can face rearwards or forwards. Larger rear pneumatic tyres, dual rear wheel-and-frame suspension and patented armadillo™ canopy are designed to make the soho suitable for all terrains and all weather. There is a full range of accessories, and it takes a Maxi-Cosi car seat.

Urban Elite, Terrain

Mountain Buggy, New Zealand
www.mountainbuggy.com

The Mountain Buggy brand began life in a garage in Auckland, New Zealand, in 1992 and has grown to attract a worldwide following among outdoor-minded parents for whom a buggy has to be good for more than a quick sprint around the shopping mall. Though many makers have now embraced the three-wheeled form, Mountain Buggy was among the first to explore this design, making their buggies more robust and versatile than many standard brands on offer at the time or now. The Mountain Buggy brand has since expanded to several styles. The Urban Elite uses smooth pneumatic tyres and rear-wheel suspension for a smooth and easy ride. Hard-wearing canvas fabric, 'the strongest buggy fabric on the market', ergonomic adjustable handlebar, swivelling, lockable front wheel and carrycot conversion are among its popular features. The Terrain, aimed at joggers, power walkers and trampers or trekkers, has a tensile aluminium frame, wide-toothed tyres and fixed front wheel for better tracking on sand or soil. Both models are available in double versions.

Orbit Infant System

Bryan White, Joseph Hei
Orbit, USA
www.orbitbaby.com

Designers Bryan White and Joseph Hei harboured ideas of designing their own products while still students at Stanford University in California before going on to work for the noted design firm IDEO. It was only after becoming parents that they decided to put their entrepreneurial dreams and considerable talents to the task of creating better-functioning products for babies and young children. After years of research and development, the Orbit Infant System was, as they say, born. We expect travel systems nowadays that allow the baby to stay in the car seat while being moved from the car to be clipped into a buggy chassis. The Orbit system has refined this interchangeable concept with their SmartHub design that not only allows a range of Orbit products (car seat, bassinet, toddler seat) to be used with their different bases (stroller, car base, rocker) but to be locked in smoothly and easily by twisting the circular hub onto the interface and then rotated to any angle. It is a high-end system, but one that offers true versatility from a comprehensive range of accessories.

BRIO Happy & Kombi

Brio, Sweden
www.brio.net

BRIO have been selling prams in Scandinavia since the 1930s, but their recent transformation of the company with 'a more contemporary edge' sees them moving into the international children's furnishings market with the Grow Highchair (see p. 74) the Colour Cot (see p. 52) and their new stroller systems. Capitalizing on recent trends for multifunctional equipment that grows in use with the child, BRIO's new signature strollers feature a pram mode (Happy) and pushchair option (Kombi) with interchangeable parts for two bases. The Compact chassis, still a substantial pram, can be folded down with wheels pulled together to a more space-saving form. With a reversible and height-adjustable handle, and EVA rubber tyres, it features the 'click-in' system for attaching the pram or seat. The Telescope chassis has a more variable telescoping handle and larger, pneumatic tyres with spoke wheels. Both models are available in a range of BRIO-designed colours.

Gecko, Cameleon, Bee

Max Barenbrug, Eduard Zanen
Bugaboo, Netherlands
www.bugaboo.com

When it launched in the UK and USA in 2001 the Bugaboo Frog caused a real stir among modern parents and others in the pram-pushing crowd. With its bold colours, high-tech details and minimalist lines it easily eclipsed most other models on the market. Conceived by industrial designer Max Barenbrug, who collaborated with physician Eduard Zanen, the Bugaboo Gecko combines advanced 'frog-like' horizontal and vertical suspension on front wheels and high manoeuvrability with a flexible design. The four wheels include two small swivels that enable it to make a perfect circle and two large, inflated, treaded tyres that add stability and handling over bumpy roads or rough terrain. The handle is height adjustable and reversible so that the larger wheels face forwards, for bumpier paths, or so that the baby can be either facing towards you or looking ahead. The frame can be fitted with a carrycot, tilting seat or car seat (made by Maxi-Cosi, see p. 14). The Cameleon can also be converted to a two-wheeled vehicle (on the two large tyres) for use on sand and snow. Tyres can be removed for storage during travel and the cot bed folded flat.

The Bee is the latest, brighter, more streamlined and portable Bugaboo with an ergonomic hard shell seat that folds down flat against the collapsed frame. Handle is still reversible and seat is adjustable. It is suitable from birth to 9 kg (19 ½ lb).

Quinny Buzz, Speedi & Zapp

Quinny/Dorel, Netherlands
www.quinny.com

The Quinny brand was established by the Quint brothers in the Netherlands before being bought by the successful conglomerate Dorel, who took the lightweight, stylish three-wheeled design and continue to improve on it. The latest version of the Buzz stroller is most remarkable for its 'gas-spring technology-one-touch opening', which allows the frame to expand at the touch of a button. The Buzz has a double swivel wheel, adjustable handle and can be used with forwards or rear-facing seat. The travel system takes a Maxi-Cosi car seat and Dreami carrycot. The Speedi model has a larger single swivel front wheel for better manoeuvrability. Its partner product, the Zapp, claims to fold to the smallest buggy in the world.

Xplory Stroller

Stokke, Norway
www.stokke.com

The thinking behind the Xplory is that 'while a number of modern strollers accommodate the growth of your child, none accommodates for their development'. The Xplory is an adjustable height stroller that allows a child to be closer physically and visually to the parent while in the protective environment of either the pram bed or the pushchair. This, say the makers, 'strengthens your child's feeling of security and comfort'. The key to the design is the central bar on which the seat or pram slides and which integrates with the handle, also adjustable for height and angle. The frame can take a pram bed, pushchair seat or certain brands of car seat. When a child is old enough to sit up, the stroller can be wheeled to the table-side and act as a high chair. Wide-spaced rear wheels allow room for comfortable walking.

Urban Rider

Mutsy B.V., Netherlands
www.mutsy.com

The Urban Rider is the most substantial of the Mutsy range, offering the stability and comfort of old-fashioned large prams with improved technology of lightweight aluminium and optional components. The Rider has large pneumatic wheels with a swivel mechanism on one axle that allows much greater manoeuvrability than with most large prams. Alternatively, one set of large wheels can be substituted with two smaller wheels that swivel individually, which is better for confined areas, such as supermarkets or public transportation. The larger wheels make the Urban Rider suitable for wooded areas or the beach, and the substantial frame can take carrycot, car seats, the twin 'duo seat' (one behind the other) and signature Mutsy 'fun seat'.

4Rider, 3Rider, Slider, Spider

Mutsy B.V., Netherlands
www.mutsy.com

With this line of strollers the designers at Mutsy have thought hard about the need for design that can be easily stored for travel on a plane or in a car boot. The 3Rider has three points of support with large pneumatic tyres for use off road and on. The 4Rider is a more compact version than the Urban Rider and is available in a single spoke or lightweight version. The travel cot, stroller seat, car seat or fun seat all fit onto the frame by means of the Mutsy 'intelligent click' system. The 4Rider also features smaller front wheels on a single swivel and folds easily with removable wheels for storage. The Slider frame consists of two separate components: the top portion with travel cot or car seat can be detached and used, for the plane or train, say, while the base folds down for storage; it also has removable wheels. The Spider is Mutsy's most compact and acrobatic model. The handle telescopes down and the seat folds backwards while front and back wheels are brought together to create a very portable stroller that comes with its own travel bag. The Spider is not as compact, but is more substantial than an umbrella stroller, as it can still be fitted with a car seat.

WIP Metrò

Edoardo Perri
WIP srl, Italy
www.wipway.com

This stroller is incredibly modern-looking, streamlined and stylish and it was designed by young talent Edoardo Perri for the re-launch of established sporting equipment manufacturers WIP in late 2007. Described as 'ultra-light and super-compact' due to a patented closing mechanism, the WIP Metrò is also bound to turn a few heads, not least because the seat can be changed to one of various available colours, or 'designed for extreme customization'. The exceedingly spare frame still makes room for an adjustable handle and 'invisible centralized brake system', which is located on the wheel and wired through the frame. The seat is made from 'climate-comfort' fabric with antibacterial memory foam with leather details. The pushchair includes a five-point safety harness not shown here. It is suitable from 6 months to 4 years.

Revolution, Ironman, Sport Utility Stroller

BOB Trailers, Inc, USA
www.bobgear.com

After you have managed to give birth to (or witnessed the birth of) one or two children, what better way to shed those extra pounds and expend that excess energy than to train for a triathlon or Ironman event, kids in tow. Catering to the growing contingent of parents with young children for whom keeping fit is a way of life, the people at BOB Trailers have made it their business to perfect the jogging pushchair. The Revolution is a lean, well-built machine with a swivel front wheel that can be locked for jogging, with three inches of suspension over off-road tyres that keep the ride smooth for the little passenger. The seat reclines up to 70 degrees with tracking adjustment to keep it all rolling straight as you keep up your pace. The Ironman Sport Utility Stroller (SUS) version is extremely lightweight, 'for the serious runner', with a fixed front wheel and fast, two-step folding. In addition to the foot-activated rear brake there is a hand-activated front brake for slowing without stopping. The wheels have 40 cm (16 in.) aluminium rims and stainless steel spokes.

Snow Baby Dream Sled

KHW, Germany
www.khw-geschwenda.de
www.3playinc.com

Created by an award-winning German manufacturer of wood and plastic products, the Snow Baby Dream Sled is one of many modern, high-tech children's sleds on the market, but unusual in its capacity as a child's pushchair. Rather than trudging a toddler through slush or trying to force the most rugged off-road stroller through snow or ice, the Snow Baby Dream Sled makes the journey from ski school to chalet easier and much more fun. Made of high-density polyethylene, with formed runners and a sturdy handle, the sled weighs 6.2 kg (14 lb), holds up to 35 kg (77 lb) and has been tested to minus 20°C (-4°F).

Smartbuggy

phil&teds, New Zealand
www.philandteds.com

While the three-wheel Sport (see opposite) suggests a more suburban ride, phil&teds Smartbuggy is definitely designed for ease of use in the urban environment. The innovative two-wheeled design is the most compact on the market and makes moving on and off public transport much easier than with a standard three or even four-wheeled buggy. This is more like just putting a couple of wheels and a sturdy harness on your child (but much more humane). When stationary, the front legs can be pulled out so that the child sits much like in a pushchair. The seat can even recline for a sleepy passenger. The front legs can then be folded in (with child still in place) and the whole thing is as easy to manage as a small shopping trolley.

Sport Single

phil&teds, New Zealand
www.philandteds.com

Leading the market for more manoeuvrable single and double buggies, phil&teds Sport uses the three-wheel, inflated tyres for a better ride and easier glide and turning. The real innovation, however, is the in-line convertible design in which the 'double kit', an additional baby seat, can be attached either at the rear and slightly below the main seat, or in front; and it can lie flat, as is best for babies. This system means the Sport can evolve from a single-seat pushchair to an upright toddler seat with baby bed, to a toddler and baby pushchair, to a vehicle that accommodates two toddlers while remaining much less bulky and yet sturdier than traditional side-by-side double buggies. The company also offer a side-by-side version, which maintains its compact yet durable stance. Simple 'click' action upgrades to double buggy, while the lightweight alloy frame and lockable swivel front wheel aid manoeuvrability. The ergonomic handle is adjustable and the double rear brake sets with a single action. Compatible with a BéBé car seat.

Wiegen Stroller

Worrell Inc, USA
www.worrell.com

Coming from the young, wide-ranging talents at
Worrell, Minneapolis, the Wiegen Stroller is a bright
spot in a growing field of innovation in pushchair,
or stroller designs. It combines the volume and depth
of an old-fashioned pram with the lightest and most
versatile new materials. But rather than carrying a
heavy-duty cot bed, the lightweight aluminium frame
supports a bed created from a unique 'stretcher
system', a neoprene enclosure with a polypropylene
support. For small babies, a sling with five-point
harness attaches to the main bed, creating a snug,
supportive cradle within the pram bed. Normally
used for wetsuits and recently for laptop covers, the
layers of neoprene effectively insulate against cold
weather, while 'snap' construction means the
neoprene can be removed easily for cleaning or
storage. This pram looks like nothing you have ever
seen carrying a baby before.

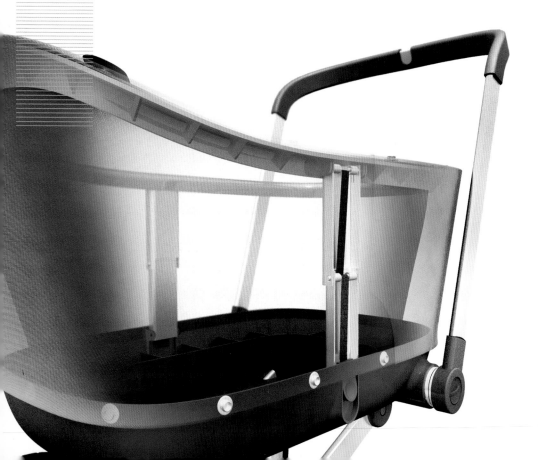

Buggypod

Stephanie Rohl
Revelo, UK
www.buggypod.com

After designer Stephanie Rohl had her second child, she says, 'I wasn't happy that the perfectly good pushchair I'd bought for my first baby was now redundant.' She wanted to continue to use the same pushchair for her new infant, though her first-born was now able to walk short distances. The answer was her design for the Buggypod, which was given a SMART award by the UK Department of Trade and Industry in 2003. The pod is really like a collapsible motorcycle sidecar for buggies. Consisting of a seat and footrest with one extra wheel, it attaches to the side of most buggies to create a temporary twin-seater. The single wheel has been given great design attention so that it does not hinder manoeuvrability, and, unlike many other wheeled attachments, can move backwards, which, Rohl points out, 'is very important when crossing busy roads'. When not in use, the Buggypod folds up against the side of the main buggy safely out of the way. Suitable from 6 months, the Buggypod is lightweight (2.5 kg/5½ lb) and compact.

X-Country Trailer

Chariot Carriers, Canada
www.chariotcarriers.com

Chariot Carriers specialize in equipment for active parents, those who want to continue hiking, jogging or cycling, with their babies or small children in tow and riding in a high degree of comfort and security. Their range of three- and four-wheeled buggies are all mountable as cycle trailers, and some are intended for 'off-road' terrain. Chariot has developed the CTS 'Child Transportation System', which allows Chariot owners to adapt their carrier to suit the chosen activity. Whether it is strolling, jogging, biking, hiking or X-Country skiing they simply need to add the attachments. All of the CTS kits are easy to install and require no tools. The X-Country series of carriers is one of their most innovative products and features CAS™ Chariot Adjustable Suspension, drum brakes on the rear wheels, generously padded interior space and removable side windows for ventilation.

Buggy Board

Lascal, Sweden
www.lascal.se
www.cheekyrascals.co.uk

One of the true innovations of the last sixteen years, the Kiddy Board brought relief to numerous parents of babies with toddlers when it launched in Sweden in 1993, and later worldwide, by allowing young walkers to hitch the occasional ride but otherwise be free of pushchair constraints. As the Kiddy Board was designed to attach to the rear axle of a buggy or pram, the company later produced the Buggy Board version, which attaches to most umbrella strollers. It has since spawned a generation of imitators and some brands, like Bugaboo (see p. 21) and Mutsy (see p. 24) now manufacture their own boards as part of their complete pushchair, or stroller travel systems.

Swiss Strolli Rider

Bibi/Lamprecht, Switzerland
www.lamprechtag.com

It is like a bike trailer for buggies. For parents with a baby and an older child not yet ready for long-distance walks, but not happy to be in a stroller, the Bibi Swiss Strolli Rider might be the answer to the awkward-walking toddler moments. It combines the fun of a bike with the stability and control of a trailer. Suitable for children from about 15 months up to 20 kg (44 lb), the Strolli has nine different adaptors to ensure that one will fit on the stroller or pushchair you own. The seat, handles and foot-rests are all adjustable.

SideCarrier

Chariot Carriers, Canada
www.chariotcarriers.com

One of the newer additions to the Chariot range is
an innovation in bike trailers. The SideCarrier can
be mounted beside the back wheel of the parent's
cycle, rather than behind it. This position allows for
better contact between parent and child during the
journey and means that the trailer takes in less road
dust. Specially designed so as not to interfere with
natural leans during turning, the SideCarrier can be
mounted to most types of adult bicycles and folded
up against the side of the bike when not in use.

Catch'em

Chariot Carriers, Canada
www.chariotcarriers.com

In line with Chariot Carriers' ethos of producing high-
quality products, all individually rather than factory
assembled, for families who enjoy being outdoors
together, the Catch'em is one of the most lightweight,
easy-to-use trailer cycles currently available. For use
by 5 to 8-year-olds, the Catch'em attaches to the rear

of an adult bike with a secure locking mechanism
which makes it easier to pull than an attached
bicycle. Featuring a lightweight aluminium frame,
the cycle has a seat and handlebars that can be easily
adjusted, and the whole frame can be folded down
without tools when not in use.

Trailerbike

Isla Rowntree
Islabikes, UK
www.islabikes.co.uk

Cyclo-cross champion Isla Rowntree established Islabikes with a thorough knowledge of cycle design and practical cycling experience to produce a range of well-designed bikes for children. Rowntree claims to have 'searched the world' for appropriate tiny components, 'and where they have not been available, has made them'. Islabikes offer a full range of cycles suitable from just over 2 years (the Rothan, see p. 186) to adult sizes. To make the cycles function well for children Rowntree ensures brakes are easily activated by small hands, and all rotating parts have ball bearings, among other specially engineered features.

The Trailerbike is a sleek companion that threatens to upstage any parent bike. Made with a full cro-moly frame, tubular steel towing rack with quick-release fitting system and safety catch, the Trailerbike also has 6-speed Shimano gears and height- and reach-adjustable aluminium handlebars.

Chunc

Richard Smith
Chunc, UK
www.chunc.com

Richard Smith was managing director of a firm that produced aeronautics components when he came up with the prototype of a new 'wheelchair for young people', based on the needs of his daughter. Smith wanted something that was 'comfortable, had a postural management seating system and was easy to use for the carers'. His new modular chair utilizes materials and engineering technology from the aerospace industry to make a wheelchair that is not only highly functional, but appealing in its modern design and bright colours. Chunc is one of the few companies catering specifically for young wheelchair users, and they now offer four versatile models with different degrees of tilt and other mobility solutions, as well as seating designed for comfort, pressure relief and improved accessibility.

Cigar, Rehab, Flex

Nihola, Denmark
www.nihola.de

The Scandinavians and the Dutch will always be one step ahead when it comes to urban solutions to cycling with small children. Danish company Nihola have been producing 3-wheeled transport for children (and goods) for many years. The Cigar is slightly more modern than other models and features a roomy compartment that can easily take two children and some shopping. It can be equipped with sun/rain canopy. Other models, the Rehab and Flex (not shown), are designed for disabled children. The Flex features a specially constructed front platform for loading a wheelchair.

Bloom

Gazelle, Netherlands
www.gazelle.nl

The Dutch are no strangers to cycling with children on board, and front-mounted seats are much more popular than in the USA or UK and often consist only of a saddle mounted onto the top bar in front of the rider without large amounts of padding or restraints. However, the cycle manufacturer Gazelle has come up with a deluxe parent bike that is ideal for fitting both a front and rear child seat. The sturdy Bloom is available in a 26-in. or 28-in. size frame and has 7 speeds with roller brakes. There is extra space between the main seat and the handle bars so that the child seat is easily accommodated. The handlebar itself is also wider. The bike can be stood up, even with panniers attached, using the double kickstand. The front wheel can be locked when the bike is standing to prevent 'clapping'. An extra long baggage carrier at the rear holds bags or child's seat. The front child seat can be fitted with its own windscreen.

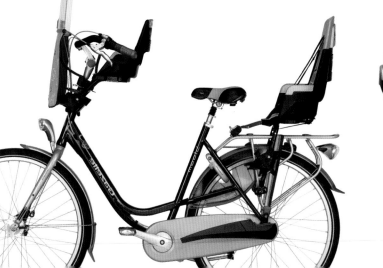

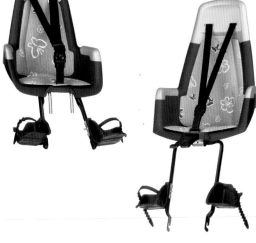

trioBike

Sammy Hessburg-Eisinger
trioBike, Denmark
www.triobike.com
www.funktionalley.com

The inspiration behind this integrated bicycle and pushchair design was a desire to 'offer a healthier, more social alternative to car travel,' according to its designer, Sammy Hessburg-Eisinger. The Danish inventor of the trioBike studied business and worked on innovative products for some of Scandinavia's largest companies before trying to help people tackle car pollution, gridlock and parking hassles with pedal power. True to its name, the trioBike has three separate functions: it operates as a bicycle-powered pushchair with a sturdy cabin that accommodates 80 kg (176 lb) of payload (or two children); as a separate, 7-speed bicycle featuring Shimano Nexus gears and lightweight aluminium frame; and as an independent pushchair with safety harnesses, disc brakes and retractable weather- and fire-proof hood. All of these alterations take minutes to achieve without tools. For example, when adding the pushchair, the front wheel twists and folds up under the carriage. Eager clients have found uses other than transporting their offspring, pets, heavy or awkward goods. London's Fifteen Restaurant delivers by trioBike. A special edition white trioBike was produced to commemorate the launch of the Scandinavian design website funktionalley.com in the spring of 2007.

Nursery

Rocking Chairs, Bassinets, Cots & Beds, Bouncers & Seats

It was the discovery that babies see and register high-contrast patterns better than soft colours that sounded the death knell for the standard nursery schemes featuring woolly lambs and teddy bears. Or maybe parents are using that fact to indulge their own taste for modern design. Either way, modern patterns and furniture design have taken hold in the nursery. And along with that is a sense of refined practicality, the knowledge that the high-design nursery furniture of the newborn days will not soon become an object of beautiful obsolescence.

The key word for the nursery of the 21st century is 'convert'. Quality, high-design furnishings come at a price, and the expense is much easier to swallow when your ideal minimalist bassinet can be changed into a handy toy bin, or a table and shelf, when the baby is ready to move into a cot. Cots that transform into child beds, changing tables that become desks, and beds that become sofas are all part of the design-led response to the fact that children grow up quickly and so the furnishings that have been chosen so carefully for them should adapt to their needs and their parents' demands for functional design.

Environmental awareness too, has had an impact on nursery furnishings, focusing both designers and parents on longevity (through adaptive designs), on wise, efficient use of natural resources and minimal reliance on chemicals or manufactured materials.

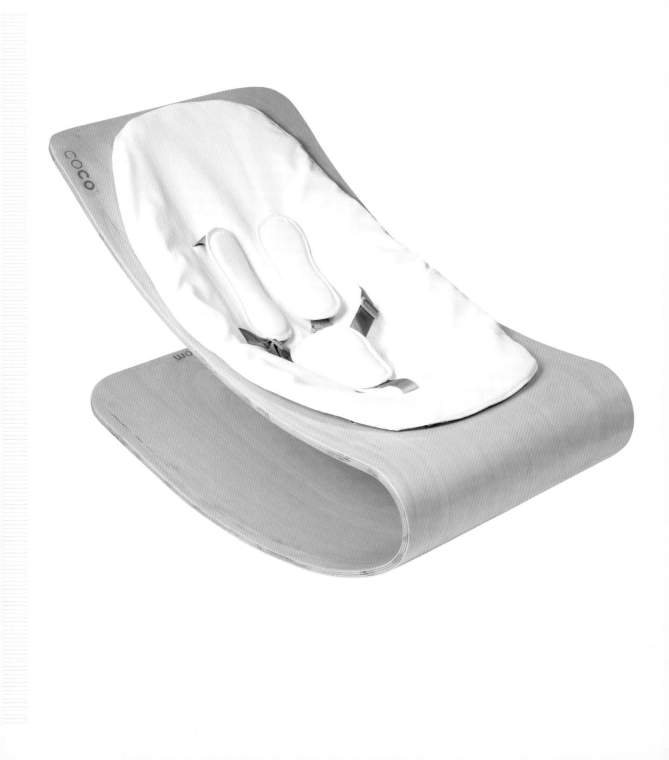

Mamma Rocking Chair

Patrick Messier
Messier Designers, Canada
www.messierdesigners.com

Industrial designer Patrick Messier worked 'on everything from aircraft interiors to furniture and consumer products to electronics and medical products' before starting his own design firm in 2002. He created the Mamma Rocking Chair as a tribute to his wife, Sophie, who was pregnant with their first child. After 'looking in vain for a rocking chair that met all our criteria,' Messier says, he decided to create one himself. The result is this delicate, flowing form, 'like a ribbon suspended in space', made from a single piece of fibreglass with a special high-gloss urethane finish. The curves are designed on a grid based on the Fibonacci sequence, but the finished chair has a less programmed, far more instinctive appeal.

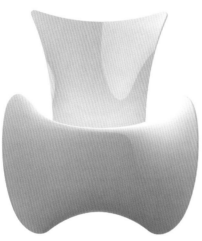

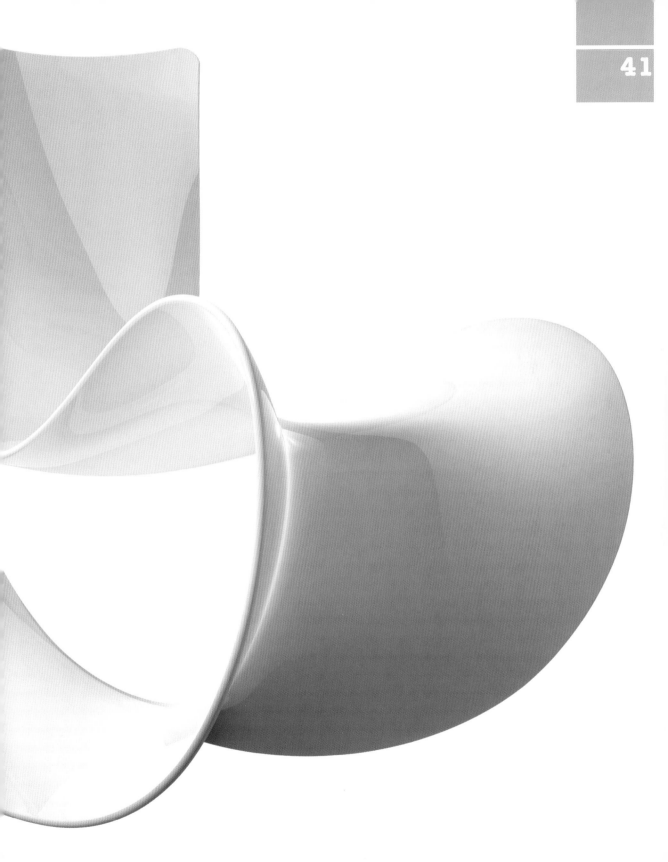

Re-tire, Re-babe, Re-mini

Tim Brauns, Hendrik Gackstatter, Fax Quintus
e27, Germany
www.e27.com

With the idea that 'the best solutions already exist somewhere', Tim Brauns, Hendrik Gackstatter and Fax Quintus have an approach of 're-thinking' existing designs to create their innovative versions. The Re-tire is a basket-woven chair on stainless-steel frame that can be joined with the Re-babe woven bassinet in the same materials, allowing the parent to rock both at once. When the baby outgrows the bassinet, the basket can be removed and replaced with a seat to make a ride-on rocking toy. For the child they also created the Re-mini rocking chair, offering something for the whole family. The chair and bassinet are available in natural or light wicker.

Goodnight Glider & Ottoman

TRUCK Product Architecture
Nurseryworks, USA
www.nurseryworks.net

The Los Angeles-based design firm Nurseryworks was founded by Traci Fleming and Kaye Popofsky Kramer, to 'celebrate the younger generation and their design-savvy parents with modern furniture, bedding, rugs, and accessories.' In addition to their own range, they offer pieces by the innovative design team TRUCK Product Architecture, such as this nursery glider and ottoman. Formed from a padded seat fitted onto a bent plywood frame the Goodnight Glider has modern lines with much-needed comfort factor and smart hues. In canvas, felt, microsuede or microterry in a range of colours.

Sleepytime Rocker

Lawson-Fenning
Nurseryworks, USA
www.nurseryworks.net

Another comfy contribution to night-time rituals
from Nurseryworks is this sturdy rocking chair with
extra wide seat for snuggling together for bedtime
stories. The design features hardwood runners with
wide upholstered seat covered in canvas, felt,
microsuede, microterry or twill in various colours.

Keinu

Eero Aarnio
Studio Eero Aarnio, Finland
www.studio-eero-aarnio.com

Finnish designer Eero Aarnio is perhaps best known
for his modern 1960s designs such as the Ball or
Globe chair. However, in recent years his playful
appeal has extended to creating children's furnishings
for Italian manufacturer Magis (see p. 106) and after
many years of refining his design for a rocking chair,
the Keinu was finally unveiled in 2003. It is a piece
of modern design that is at home in the most
discriminating of collections.

Baby Hammock

Baby Hammock
Babylonia, Belgium
www.babylonia.be

There is no question that babies sleep better when
swaddled; most new parents are rather startled
when they first place their newborn in a cot where
they seem to float in an overlarge space. The Baby
Hammock keeps babies snug and supports them in
a comfortable, beneficial, semi-curled position. Made
from 100 per cent unbleached cotton, the hammock
ties to the ends of a cot or playpen. Recommended
for use from 0 to 4 months.

Eco Cradle

Ruth Kenan
Green Lullaby, Israel
www.green-lullaby.com

Among her cardboard creations
for children (see p. 120), designer
Ruth Kenan has created the
ultimate portable and recyclable
baby bed. Made of recycled material,
the cardboard cradle has been
treated with an eco-friendly, non-
toxic fire retardant and meets
European safety standards. It is
lightweight, foldable and can be
assembled or disassembled in
seconds. The cradle is available
in three colours.

Knoppa Cradle

Anna Häggblom, Ola Stålhammer
Sfär, Sweden
www.sfaer.se

The hanging cradle is returning to popularity, certainly in Scandinavia, both for reasons of comfort and space. The snug environment created for babies helps to make them feel secure and calm, according to experts. The cradle can be mounted as a hanging basket from a ceiling loop with a carbine hook and cleat located at the juncture of the four wire stays. It can be anchored with an additional hook fixed on the wall. The cradle is suspended on a 6 mm thick stainless-steel wire and can be adjusted to any height and moved in a gentle swaying motion. Designer Anna Häggblom trained and works as a graphic designer and has published books on textile printing. Established interior designers, she and her husband created the Knoppa Cradle when they lived in a small apartment and their second child was not sleeping well. According to Häggblom, 'it worked very well'. Now others are benefitting from their experiment. Consult a specialist hardware supplier for fixings. The cradle support weighs up to 30 kg (66 lb). At the time of writing the designers were developing designs for easier hanging and height adjustment mechanisms.

Leander Cradle

Stig Leander Nielsen
Leanderform, Denmark
www.leanderform.dk

Craftsman and designer Stig Leander Nielsen looks to classic Danish
furniture before creating his modern interpretations. The Leander
Cradle has an old-fashioned appeal while retaining a clean, simple shape
with high-quality cotton fitted onto a metal frame. The cradle can then
be hung from the ceiling or from the specially designed wood tripod.
Leander Nielsen believes in physical modelling to create his products
with respect to detail. He has followed up the cradle with an award-
winning cot/child bed design (see p. 53) and high chair (see p. 68).

Ninna-Nanna Bassinet

Ralph Montemurro
Monte Design Group, Canada
www.montedesign.net

According to Ralph Montemurro of Monte Design, 'ninna-nanna comes from an old Italian song parents sing to their children while putting them to sleep.' The bassinet is made of a removable basket that sets into a solid wood rocker base of Canadian maple. The padded sides are covered with a removable, machine-washable suede microfibre that is water repellent and stain resistant. Montemurro founded Monte Design Group with his wife, Michelle, after they had children and found that 'there was such a tremendous void in the market for attractive nursery furnishings.' Though he had previously worked mostly in sportswear design, Montemurro nurtured a lifelong passion for modern furniture. With products like the Ninna-Nanna Bassinet he maintains a seasoned 'eye for excellent fabrics and quality stitching' as well as the company's focus on largely natural materials, clean lines and superior quality. The bassinet is handmade.

Oberon Cradle

Nature's Sway
Moffii Ltd, UK
www.moffii.com

Age-old swaddling has been rediscovered by New Zealand company Nature's Sway, who rebranded the stork bundle for modern parents. It was imported by Moffii in the UK, who commissioned the Oberon frame from Adam White of Factory Design to create the Moffii Oberon. The naturally snug pull of the gathered fabric cradles the infant, giving babies the closeness and feeling of security that they crave. The cradle is made of undyed organic cotton fabric. The baby can also be gently rocked in its soft enclosure.

YiAhn Bassinet

Chul Min Kang
industREALdesign, USA
www.yiahn.com

Following close on the success of his Min chair (see p. 127), industrial designer Chul Min Kang designed this versatile bassinet system for his son, YiAhn. The sectional design means that the components can be taken apart and reformed into a toy bin and shelves or a chair and table once the bassinet is no longer needed. It is made of Plyboo®, a laminated bamboo plywood made from renewable bamboo, using adhesives that are strong and low-emitting. The interior fabric is 100 per cent undyed cotton fastened with Velcro at each end. Drawers in the bottom provide storage for nappies or diapers and changing products.

Seimi Bassinet

Leena Peltonen
Seimi, Finland
www.seimi.fi

Meri Peltonen and her husband, Olli Helanto, were
already established designers of custom interiors and
handcrafted wood furnishings when they launched
the Seimi collection after the birth of their daughter,
Ines, in 2002. Meri later asked her interior designer
parents to join the team and their first products were
welcomed with immediate praise in Scandinavian
design shows. The bassinet follows the Seimi principles
of pure design, using natural, joined birch or oak
with open-weave fabric in a choice of neutral colours.
The bassinet can be folded down for travel or storage.
From 0-6 months.

Ovum Bassinet

Heidi Newell
Offi, USA
www.offi.com

Designer Heidi Newell's concept for a compact
bassinet came from the appeal of Shaker furniture;
particularly, it seems, the rounded wooden boxes. The
Ovum is two ovoid shapes in bent ply that can be set
stably one atop the other or with the bottom oval on
its side to create a rocker. The angled shape of the top
bed portion is meant to ensure that the baby can be
seen from any angle in the room. The bassinet was
greeted with excitement among children's furniture
dealers at its launch in 2007 for the winning
combination of simplicity and innovation. 'We wanted
to communicate the care, joy and wisdom that modern
parents have for their newborns,' says the designer.
The bassinet is available in dark or light wood.

Founder of Chicago-based children's furniture company Ooba, Scott Wilson is the former Global Creative Director for Nike and Design Director for Motorola. He has produced award-winning furniture and product designs in addition to his designs for children, and has gained an international following for such innovative products as the Nike eyeD body performance monitor and the OTTO chair for Moroso, which is in the Mercedes-Benz Museum, Stuttgart.

'Great design is the balance of function and form, thought and emotion.'

Above. Ooba Bassinet by Scott Wilson.

Do you have a favourite children's design object, toy or piece of furniture whether from your own childhood or a recent product, and why does it appeal to you?

That is tough. I guess that falls under 'nothing is good enough for your kids'. I really don't like anything in particular that is 'designed'. Stuff that tries too hard to be modern and is over-designed doesn't do it for me. Maybe there is something still lacking in the category. I think Lego still has me. I like how they have evolved. It is an engaging product for both kids and adults which promotes closer interaction and enjoyment between adult and child. Play-doh™ is still great as well.

If design is supposed to be largely functional, what is the function of play in design?

Great design is the balance of function and form, thought and emotion. Much like human relationships, beauty without substance results in a brief interest and infatuation. Products that deliver on both levels build a strong relationship with the user and a brand loyalty. Play is obviously the emotional side of the product experience when it comes to toys. Play should be about freedom, creativity and imagination.

What is the most difficult aspect of designing for kids?

Well, safety has to be at the top of the list. To maintain and balance safety with purity of form, manufacturability, ease of assembly, and cost is the biggest challenge.

Given that a child's perception is much more 'pure' than that of an adult jaded by decades of consumerism, is it possible for a child to differentiate between 'design', 'experience' and 'emotion'?

Children are drawn in by pure emotional connection and if the experience is good, then it is good. There is no rationalizing or convincing them to like something. To a certain extent being able to see things through the

eyes of a child is a very valuable skill for a designer. And parents have little tolerance for anything inferior when it comes to their children.

What product or existing piece of design would you most like to redesign for children?
The glider [armchair rocker], without a doubt. It may be an American nursery staple but it is a horrible piece of furniture that possesses a taste-defying must-have soothing motion. There is still much to be desired about most of the category. There is more design activity today in the industry, but very few icons that will stand the test of time.

'Much of the physical fluff produced today lacks substance and fails to register with many children for more than a day.'

In an age of instant digital gratification, what do you think is the most important consideration in designing for kids today?
It is tough to compete with digital gratification. The key once again is balance. There is substantial benefit from some digital tools and experiences. However, technology cannot replace engaging physical and spatial interaction. I think well-designed interactions and physical toys from ten or twenty years ago are still valid and can be evolved and built upon. Much of the physical fluff produced today lacks substance and fails to register with many children for more than a day. And, of course, it is still hard to beat the ball, the crayon, the cardboard box, and quality time with parents. Children will turn more and more to digital media when time-challenged parents are not available.

Modernist-inspired products for kids are sometimes criticized for trying to appeal more to design-savvy parents than to children. Do you think this is true and if so, is it such a bad thing?
I think modernism and juvenile design share some very similar attributes but, in large, are very misaligned. Both reduce objects down to their essence ('less is more'). Both can have bold, colourful designs, though the juvenile palette is somewhat expected and stagnant. Seemingly it would be easy for both to comfortably coexist.

Alex

ducduc
ducduc, USA
www.ducducnyc.com

The Alex crib comes in a range of colours, including white, pink, blue and natural, as well as bold orange. It is made of hardwood with four mattress settings to accommodate growing children and the adults who have to lift and settle them. One of ducduc's more basic designs, Alex has a matching dresser/changing table with finger-hole drawer pulls and a removable changing tray.

BRIO Colour Cot

BRIO, Sweden
www.brio.net

Part of BRIO's new contemporary line of children's furnishings brought out in 2007 (see pp. 20, 70), the Colour Cot is meant to be a high-quality classic cot 'in modern funky colours.' It is adjustable to two levels and available in red, green or white.

Leander Bed

Stig Leander Nielsen
Leanderform, Denmark
www.leanderform.dk

The award-winning Leander Bed grows from baby
to toddler to young child, and maintains the graceful
curved form that demonstrates the designer's
homage to classic Danish design. Made of form-
shaped beech, the cot can be converted by taking
down the rails and leaving the high head and
footboards, and then by reducing the ends and
extending the length to create a very simple,
functional and beautiful piece of furniture.

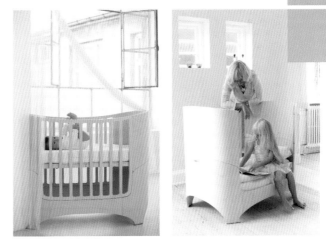

Care, Sleepi

Stokke, Norway
www.stokke.com

Norwegian makers Stokke have been in the business of producing fine children's furnishings for many years. Their soft-curved forms in natural wood are easy to spot and combine simplicity with practicality that is hard to beat. Their nursery range is well-aimed at babies, but also transforms to early years' furniture and beyond with some surprising results. The Sleepi cot has a friendly ovoid shape and can be hung with a soft canopy for young babies. Later it converts to a toddler bed and daybed, while the Care changing table with its handy array of shelves breaks down to create a child's desk perfectly matched with a junior Tripp Trapp chair (see p. 75). Made of cultivated beech, the pair come in a range of natural varnishes and with pivoting lockable wheels.

Nest Crib & Bassinet

Scott Wilson
Ooba, USA
www.ooba.com

As former Global Creative Director at Nike and Design Director at Motorola, Scott Wilson knows his way around the design market, and vows to create his furnishings range with a childlike vision but also with 'uncompromising style'. In his own-brand Ooba Nest collection he has combined sleek, minimalist aesthetics with demands for comfort and practicality. The Nest Crib and Bassinet both feature the stylish surface combinations of smooth bent wood and clean white chrome metal. Free of fussy ornament or funky detailing, the cool designs highlight the 'ooooh' in Ooba and will attract many a modernist admirer. However, they also offer high-quality materials and clever transformation appeal. The crib converts to a toddler daybed; while the bassinet can be made into a separate play table (with added top) and toy bin (with added feet).

Loft Changing Table, Crib & Dresser

David Netto
Netto Collection, USA
www.nettocollection.com

When David Netto, designer of chic interiors, became a father in 2001, he lamented the lack of stylish nursery furniture. 'There was no modern,' he says, 'there was no luxury. There was definitely nothing that offered both.' Teaming up with textiles designer Lulu de Kwiatkowski, he created the Netto Collection, a range of nursery furnishing for the style-conscious home that not only bring a little taste into the baby's room, but are designed to extend and grow as the baby becomes a toddler, a pre-schooler, even a school-age child. The Loft Collection, inspired by mid-century modernist design, features clean lines, solid ash and white lacquer finish and stainless steel. Changing table partitions can be removed, as can the top tray, and the unit can be used as a side table. The Loft Crib converts to an open-sided daybed with storage baskets below.

Dylan

David Harris, Brady Wilcox
ducduc, New York
www.ducducnyc.com

The collaborative design house of ducduc have taken the theme of adaptable furniture to new heights of style and comfort with their ranges for children's rooms and nurseries. The Dylan line embraces a simple modular approach and the clean finish of white-painted hardwood (no MDF is used). All of the bases include drawers with interiors painted in brightly contrasting orange to match the mattresses for the crib and bonding bench®. The bench is meant to provide a space for parents to sit close by and/or play in the early years. Later on the bench can be used as a stand-alone ottoman or the cushion can be removed and used in the crib (transformed to a daybed), 'leaving you', say the designers, 'with a beautiful clean cocktail table'. The cot can be converted to a toddler bed and then to a modernist-style daybed, or, using optional extensions, to a full-size platform bed. The dresser is designed for use as a changing table connected to the other elements, but can also be separated from the rear storage plinth and used on its own. The plinth has a cut-out shelf or can function as a twin-size headboard.

Classic Mini Library, Cot & Toddler Bed

Sophie Demenge, Michael Ryan
Oeuf, USA
www.oeufnyc.com

Husband-and-wife team Sophie Demenge and Michael Ryan founded their first design company, R+D Design, in 1999, making furniture and home accessories. In 2002, after becoming parents, they started their children's venture, Oeuf, concentrating on producing 'practical and stylish essentials' for 'design-conscious and environmentally aware parents'. Their basic range is a clean-lined collection for the nursery with simple, shaped details. It includes a cot, or crib, that converts to a toddler bed with side rails and mini library and changing table. The cot sides, and head and footboarda are made from single panels of wood, so there are no vulnerable joints. They are of Baltic birch and environmentally friendly MDF.

Studio Crib

TRUCK Product Architecture
Nurseryworks, USA
www.nurseryworks.net

Los Angeles-based Nurseryworks has become a leading American brand of fine furnishings for babies and children. Founders Traci Fleming and Kaye Popofsky Kramer work in collaboration with select partners, such as TRUCK Product Architecture who created the crib shown here. The Studio Crib makes one piece of furniture multi-task by including a fold-out changing table with storage cupboard below as well as a storage drawer under the bed. When the cot is converted to a toddler bed the changing table can be used as a desk or display table. The frame is made of catalpa or zebra wood; it takes a standard crib-size mattress.

Orbit Bassinet Cradle & Rocker Base

Orbit Baby, USA
www.orbitbaby.com

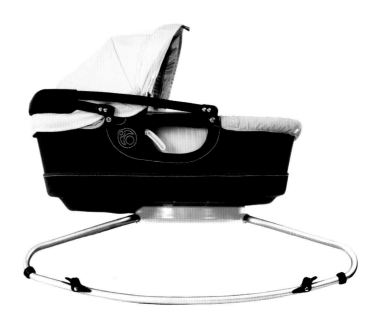

One of the latest offerings in the Orbit range is the Bassinet Cradle carry cot, which includes a light-weight rocker frame. Fitted with the Orbit SmartHub dock, the frame can also be used with the Orbit Infant Car Seat (see p. 12) or Toddler Seat to form a rocker or bouncer seat. The bent metal frame can be rocked or bounced gently; the bassinet can swivel forwards or in a side-to-side motion.

Bumbo Baby Sitter

Johan Buitendach
Bumbo, South Africa
www.bumbobabysitter.com

The Bumbo Baby Sitter seat was developed to allow younger babies to sit up and explore their environment in a secure position, instead of lying back in a reclining position. It can be used as soon as a baby can hold his or her head up without assistance. The dug-out seat and soft, low-density foam construction make it balanced and sturdy enough to support babies in a comfortable upright position. The makers cite its many ergonomic design assets, including providing correct support for the lumbar region. It is recommended for special needs babies, for sitting upright is not only an aid to digestion but to perception and other functions. The Bumbo seat also makes a stable feeding chair and a lightweight, portable toddler seat. It comes in a range of colours.

Babysitter Frame

Mutsy B.V., Netherlands
www.mutsy.com

If verstility and flexibility are watchwords for modern children's products then Dutch brand Mutsy's product relaunch for 2007 marked a thoroughly modern remake. Featuring three car seats, a cot bed, a twin seat and pushchair, or stroller, seat that all fit into the four Mutsy stroller frames, the line also presents a simple and incredibly useful frame that becomes a baby-seat or bouncer when fitted with a seat. Keeping the detailing and component parts the same makes for a wealth of options within one stylistic and mechanistic vocabulary. In short, it simplifies life. The stroller seat can be set upright on the frame and stabilized with a tray for feeding or reclined for rocking and sleeping.

LazyTed

phil&teds, New Zealand
www.philandteds.com

Those daring designers at phil&teds seem to keep pushing boundaries with new and ever more adaptable products, as their motto 'adapt and survive' becomes ever more appropriate. The LazyTed bouncer is one of the more recent additions to their catalogue. It works as a streamlined modern bouncer by using the seat from the 'double kit' (which converts the Sport Single pushchair or stroller to a double by attaching to the front or rear of the chassis) on the powder-coated metal bouncer frame. The robust structure can also be used as a toddler seat. The LazyTed is available in seven colours.

Doomoo Seat

Delta Diffusion, Belgium
www.doomoo.be

This is a colourful beanbag for
babies. The basic angled shape
is similar to ordinary bouncers,
but the Doomoo Seat certainly
looks and feels a lot more
comfortable. The seat comes with
two removable top layer options,
one that includes a safety harness
for babies and one plain upper
layer for older children. Developed
as part of the Doomoo range of
soft support pillows and bolsters
for sleeping, resting, breastfeeding
and lounging about, the seat is
filled with microballs and covered
in soft, stretchy microfibre with
a washable top layer. Doomoo
Seat is suitable from birth up to
approximately 30 kg (66 lb).

Coco Baby Lounger

bloom, Hong Kong, USA, Europe
www.bloombaby.com

Another product from the
company started by the innovative
'four dads' (see p. 18), who
launched their company in 2006,
the Coco Baby Lounger has a
streamlined, contemporary design
using patented stylewood™ or
plexistyle™ and covered in soft
microsuede™ or leatherette™. In
2008 they launched the ei (ebony
and ivory) collection featuring
black and white colours, for a
truly modern, stylish start in life.

Babyswing

Johannes Mohr
Mohr Polster, Austria
www.mohrpolster.at

Johannes Mohr's upholstery company does new work and restoration,
including specialized small series designs for clients such as Peter
Zumthor. In 2001 he created the felt swing for his baby daughter. Made
of 5 mm-thick wool felt, it holds a baby snugly like a baby carrier and is
suspended by ropes for gentle swinging but not for bouncing. The
Babyswing is available in assorted colours.

Bouncer

Kjell Hagstrom, Fredrik Almander
Svan, Sweden
www.svan.se
www.svanstore.com

Svan, Swedish for 'Swan', began with the now-iconic design for a high chair, whose S-shape in pure birch wood recalls the elegant shape of the water bird. Founding designers, Kjell Hagstrom and Anders Fallman, have expanded the brand to include their Mini Furniture, Scooter and Bouncer all made of smooth bent wood. The Bouncer maintains the curved lines of the chair, is fully height adjustable and can be used with a hood for sleeping babies. The seat bounces with the baby's own movement and can be collapsed for storage. The seat is detachable, and of machine-washable fabric. For use up to 13.5 kg (30 lb).

Baby Sitter 1-2-3

BabyBjörn, Sweden
www.babybjorn.com

The Swedish company began in 1961 with the design of their first baby carrier, which they have continued to improve on (see pp. 215, 224) and were one of the first companies to be considered really 'modern' in their approach to childcare products. The Baby Sitter 1-2-3 is a good example of a basic piece of equipment that has been improved while being allowed to remain pleasingly simple. The sturdy but lightweight metal frame has three positions ('play, rest and sleep') and can be folded down for storage or transport. Anti-skid pads keep the sitter in place when the child bounces, and protect floors from scuffs. The fabric is reversible and machine washable, and the restraint and toy belt can be removed when the baby is old enough to get in and out of the seat by themselves.

Mealtimes

Highchairs, Utensils

Mealtimes with children and babies can be a tricky business. Fraught or funny, and usually messy, they are often not as peaceful as we would like. Even in families with children already, a baby at the table throws the dynamic considerably, so good design in the necessary elements – highchairs, plates, cutlery – can help make those trying culinary moments a little more palatable for everyone.

Highchairs are essential, and it is no longer necessary to accommodate an awkward plastic chair decorated in gaudy vinyl that cracks or catches food in its seams. Simple designs in wood, metal and revolutionary plastics are being used to create chairs that are easy to manoeuvre, fold away, or, in some cases, spin around to face different directions. Some are height adjustable and several now can evolve for use with growing children even to the point of being functional and comfortable for adults. Most new chairs have removable trays that facilitate cleaning but, with the tray absent, also offer the option of bringing the child up to the table as part of the process of learning to eat alongside and as part of the family.

Designs in children's tableware reflect research into how small children grasp and hold objects. Some designers use child-friendly shapes in finer materials, like stainless steel and porcelain. Others go for vibrant colour assortments in melamine and polypropylene. Since young children investigate the objects around them, it makes sense to offer them something that satisfies as many senses as possible.

Leander Highchair

Stig Leander Nielsen
Leanderform, Denmark
www.leanderform.dk

2007 was a busy year for Stig Leander Nielsen. Having recently launched his designs for a hanging cradle (see p. 46) and convertible cot bed (see p. 53), he then turned his hand to the design of another basic piece of baby kit. The Leander Highchair exhibits a familiar Scandinavian predilection for solid craftsmanship, pure forms and natural wood, while also offering distinctive details and a spirited palette of cushion colours. The chair is designed for babies upwards.

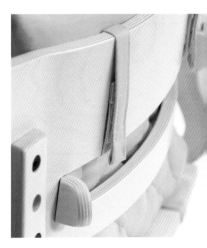

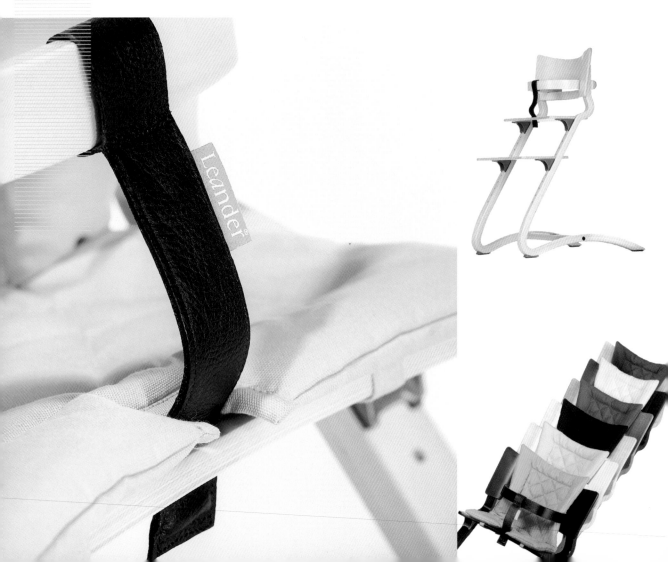

HiLo Kids' Chair

Patrice Guillemin, Geneviève Grenier
AGEDesign, Canada
www.agedesign.ca

Husband and wife design team of Patrice Guillemin and Geneviève Grenier went to work on a new highchair design after the birth of their son Arthur in 2005. Their aim was to make something 'easy to adjust, easy to clean, easy to use and nice to look at.' The HiLo Kids' chair is all these things and a unique contribution to the range of highchairs currently available. The robust moulded plastic seat (HDPE with lead-free pigmentation), set in a frame of chunky 20-ply beech veneer and hand-machined solid aluminium hardware, flips around from baby height to child level. The wood tray can be removed for cleaning and when pulling the chair up to the table. For children of 6 months to 6 years, the HiLo is made in Canada and comes with a book of home recipes.

Fresco Contemporary Baby Chair, Nano Folding Highchair

bloom, Hong Kong, USA, Europe
www.bloombaby.com

The 'four dads' who founded bloom (see p. 18) came up with an award-winning highchair in 2006. The fresco takes the newly popular pedestal barber-chair style and adds a twist of versatility and bold colour. The seat is on a pneumatic-assist device for raising and lowering, and rotates 360 degrees to help parents get children in and out of the chair more easily and move them to a better feeding position. The seat also reclines to work as a daytime bed for newborns and young babies. The footrest is adjustable and the chair can be used with a tray, bar or as an open-access child seat. For parents who have to cope with limited kitchen space, bloom has improved on and simplified the folding highchair. The Nano's curved legs and ovoid shape create a neatly folded object without any awkward edges. Opened for use, the Nano is a graceful object that maintains the bloom sense of colour and style.

The Table, Bench, Booster Seat & Highchair

ducduc, USA
www.ducducnyc.com

Describing themselves as 'a collaborative design house that creates quality products for children', ducduc have emerged as producers of some of the most stylish furnishings for children, or more accurately, for families with children, in the USA. If the key to enticing families to invest in high-quality children's furniture is to make products that last longer (in terms of quality) and that adapt as children grow older (grow with them), then ducduc should be very successful. The dining table is a masterpiece in adaptable modern family design. The combination of walnut and white-painted board in sleek modular sections speaks of real modernist principles of materials and form. The benches and table both contain storage, and the design includes a highchair and booster seat additions that fit onto the benches, while the table panels slide out so that children can reach more easily. The whole design is one of calm efficiency. It is upholstered in patented Crypton fabric, which has been engineered to be stain, water and bacteria resistant. All finishes are non-toxic. Sliding table panels are walnut on one side but can be flipped over to reveal whiteboard, which children can write on.

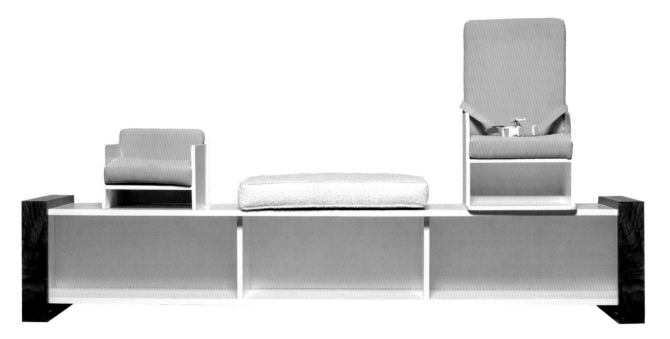

Grow-up Booster Seat

Mutsy B.V., Netherlands
www.mutsy.com

Another bright and bold offering from Dutch company Mutsy, this is a modern take on the old booster seat. The PUR foam seat reducer fits into a hard plastic base that stays put in a regular dining chair using safety straps. The seat reducer can also be used with the Mutsy Easygrow Highchair. It is designed for use for children up to 4 years.

Easygrow Highchair

Mutsy B.V., Netherlands
www.mutsy.com

The Easygrow is a slim-line anodized aluminium frame with translucent plastic seat and back that would look at home in any clean-line modern or industrial interior. Add the adjustable footrest, tray, bumper bar and seat reducer and you have a fully flexible baby-to-child highchair. The chair is available in five colours.

Nest

Sally Dominguez
Mozzee, Australia
www.mozzee.co.uk

It might have the look of a bit of scenery from a sci-fi film set, but the Nest by Mozzee is a new, award-winning highchair that converts to a funky toddler TV seat. The weighted tulip-shaped base minimizes tripping hazards in busy kitchens and allows the chair to be pulled right up to the table. It also makes for a remarkably stable highchair. The seamless hemisphere seat made of UV stabilized polyethelene has no hidden cracks or crevices to trap food and can be easily wiped down in its entirety. Its 'scooped' shape means that children are reclined slightly and, say the designers, are comfortable for longer periods. The removable tray is also easy to clean. The conversion kit turns the Nest into the Nester, a slick, comfortable, child-sized low chair. The Nest is available in white or orange.

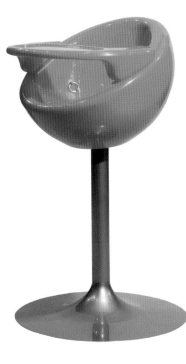

BRIO Grow Highchair

Mia Korpi
BRIO, Sweden
www.brio.net

BRIO's launch of a line of children's accessories in 2006-7 marked the company's move to cater to a new generation of parents who, the company say, want to have it all, 'travel, live in style and have rewarding careers while still providing the best for their children'. They approached designer Mia Korpi at the School of Design in Göteborg to develop the first BRIO highchair and she came up with the striking shape of the Grow, made from bent wood with a chrome base and a removable soft (compact foam) cushion in orange/white and black/white as well as plain white. The foam seat can be changed when a new colour is desired.

Flair Elite Pedestal Highchair

Rebecca Finell
Boon, USA
www.booninc.com

When you think of barber shops and hair salons, you wonder why no one thought of this before, since a lot of the work of looking after small children has to do with lifting and moving them. The Flair highchair was developed by industrial designer and parent Rebecca Finell, who had her first success with the Frog Pod bath-toy caddy (see p. 243) and formed her company, Boon, with Ryan Fernandez. The Flair combines the easy cleaning and streamlined design of a seamless moulded plastic seat with the mechanics of a pneumatic lift and sturdy pedestal base. The seat has a removable pad and the tray has a cover that can go in the dishwasher. Six castors fitted under the base mean that the chair can be wheeled around the kitchen as needed, and a foot brake locks them in place for stability. The Elite model features a stainless steel base, high-gloss white seat and choice of colours for the seat pad.

Tripp Trapp Chair

Peter Opsvik
Stokke, Norway
www.stokke.com

When Peter Opsvik developed this design in the late 1970s, it was a true innovation in children's highchairs. Being fully adjustable so that it could 'grow with the child', it could be said to be the product that launched a new interest in quality children's products that appeal to a (grown-up) modernist-influenced aesthetic. The solid wood original was easy to assemble, adjust and re-assemble, and was as comfortable for an adult or older child as it was for a baby. But this was not just a piece of high-end design aimed at parents. Opsvik considered the child's comfort first, allowing them to 'sit at the table in a natural way with the family', and adding the movable footrest so the child experiences the security of having their feet supported (as adults do when they sit). The chair also allows older children to sit with their elbows at table height and their feet supported. Opsvik and Stokke have since improved on the chair, offering a variety of infant pads and a range of colours, but kept the incredibly efficient, stable and popular zigzag shape.

Calla Highchair

Yves Béhar
Fleurville, USA
www.fleurville.com

Founder of innovative San Francisco-based design group Fuseproject,
Swiss-born designer Yves Béhar has become one of the most influential
designers of his generation. With a portfolio that includes ground-
breaking projects for Nike, Microsoft, Herman Miller and Toshiba,
he seems the ideal candidate, as a recent father, to re-invent children's
design, starting with the highchair. His aim was to enhance the
interaction between parents and infants: 'I wanted it without corner, a
big round friendly space where kids can wave their hands and parents
can get in close without hitting their knees on the legs.' The ergonomic
design does these things as well as providing an adjustable 'stem' to
meet the table height, removable seat cushion, detachable, dishwasher-
safe tray and wide, wheeled base for stability and flexibility. Then there
is the welcoming form of the Calla Lily, with the child nestled in a
rounded trumpet-flower blossom, all round and friendly.

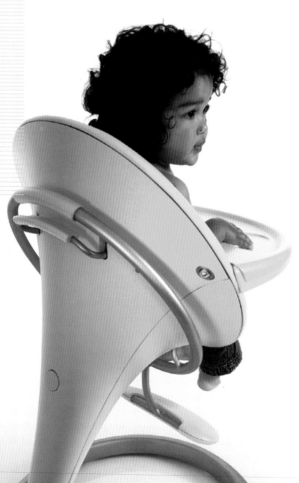

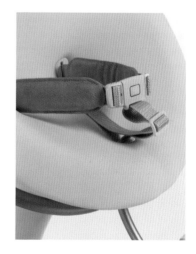

K2 Highchair

Steve Küster
Küster, UK
www.kuster.co.uk

A graduate of London's Royal College of Art, Steve Küster has been on a mission to create 'products with innovation, style and functionality' for children (see also p. 242). The folding K2 is no mountain to climb, but a highchair that is ergonomically designed and a very modern-looking addition to the kitchen. Made of wood and chrome, it has a minimal presence, though it is made to accommodate children from 6 months up to 6 years. The wipe-clean tray also has an optional protective cover. Feet are adjustable to mediate uneven floor surfaces and maintain a secure stance. Cushions in lively contemporary print patterns are available separately.

Carota

Toshimitsu Sasaki
Sasaki Design International, Japan
www.sdii.jp

Award-winning product and furniture designer Toshimitsu Sasaki created his Fantasia line of children's furniture in 2004 for his own children after experimenting for many years with handmade furniture on his own. Sadly, Sasaki died in 2005, but the design studio, run by members of the Sasaki family, carries on the creation of such modern craftsman-like pieces as the Carota chair, which can be used as a highchair or lowered for a children's table height. The chair is made of bent wood, having a birch core with maple veneer.

Child/Child Highchair & Chair

Maartje Steenkamp
Studio Maartje Steenkamp, Netherlands
www.maartjesteenkamp.nl

Maartje Steenkamp was inspired by her own children to improve on existing children's products. The white beechwood Highchair with extra long legs was designed with the idea that a small child likes to be carried around and observe the world on the same eye level as the parent. As the child grows, the legs can be sawed shorter (Steenkamp provides measurement markers for guidance on the legs, as well as the necessary saw). The birch ply Child/Child Chair evolved from an earlier Mother/Child seat-and-table construction that was based on Steenkamp's own body measurements and reach. This version allows siblings to sit safely together and interact at mealtimes or play.

Rinki

Hannu Peltonen
Seimi, Finland
www.seimi.fi

Another award-winning pure design product from Seimi, Finland, the Rinki highchair is a simple form that converts from stool to highchair with a minimum of components or fuss. Made of solid birch with a seat and guard ring available in a choice of five colours, the stool is 56.5 cm (22 in.) while the chair is 72.5 cm (28 ½ in.) high. The Rinki and Seimi bassinet (see p. 49) are part of a range of natural wood baby furnishings created by the family design firm Seimi.

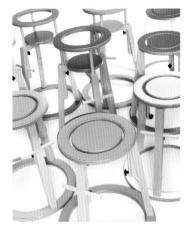

Yves Béhar is a leading internationally recognized product designer and Creative Director of Fuseproject, a multi-disciplinary creative firm based in San Francisco. Among his highly lauded recent designs is the Leaf light for Herman Miller. He recently began designing for children and has produced the Calla highchair and Y Water. He designed the portable, battery-powered laptop for One Laptop Per Child, an educational initiative spearheaded by Nicholas Negroponte to provide laptop computers for children in the developing world. To date 400,000 units have been shipped to different countries and 250,000 more have been provided through the Give1 Get 1 campaign.

'...we have a particular responsibility to speak to the kids' intelligence...'

Above middle / Above / Right.
One Laptop Per Child by Yves Béhar.

Given that a child's perception is much more 'pure' than that of an adult jaded by decades of consumerism, is it possible for a child to differentiate between 'design', 'experience' and 'emotion'?

I think kids differentiate between all these aspects on an intuitive level. Their experiences are deep, and less superficial than ours. For that reason, we have a particular responsibility to speak to the kids' intelligence, sustain their interest, find ways to not add to the disposability of consumerism, and contribute to their longterm development. When working on the Calla highchair, a child psychologist did inform me that exposing kids to quality in the things they play and learn with, makes them seek quality in other products and experiences later in life. This is a fact never to forget when designing for kids.

What product or existing piece of design would you most like to redesign for children?

So many! I recently had a little boy, and I have the desire to redesign many of the products that he experiences: from the everyday nappies or diapers, to playpens, cots, cribs etc...

In an age of instant digital gratification, what do you think is the most important consideration in designing for kids today?

Quality is a cornerstone of kids' early experience and their future, so the physical and tactile world needs to be designed to the highest standards for them in order for have a society that will continue to evolve towards a better world.

What is your favourite object for children, whether a toy you had as a child or something new you have discovered?

Enzo Mari's puzzles, '16 animali' and '16 pesci', designed for Danese, because of the quality and beauty of the shapes, the natural wood, the modularity and creative play possibilities, and the poetry of the story.

Kids' Stuff Tableware, Glasses & Cutlery

Alfredo Häberli
Iittala, Finland
www.iittala.com

Alfredo Häberli's design for a set of children's tableware including glasses and cutlery was, he says, 'one of my favourite projects of the last few years'. His belief is that designing for children is not about making something 'twenty percent smaller, or applying childish fantasies, but finding the playful element in each component'. Looking at his Kids' Stuff range it is easy to see that he has little time for fanciful figures, yet the shapes and colours are satisfying enough in their way. The cutlery is sized appropriately, but still functional and easy to handle; the plates are ceramic, with deep rimmed edges to help minimize spilling, and the glassware looks like something a grown-up would use, but can be held firmly with small hands. The collection also includes plastic trays and a wooden cutting board.

Silver Spoon

Aprica, Italy
www.aprica-italia.it

It may seem like a move of unabashed marketing to offer a baby utensil in the form of a company logo, but this particular piece of baby tableware is so lovely to look at and to hold, and so unobviously a brand, that it cannot be bad to offer it to little ones for inspection and possible table practice. The smallest is a charm that can be added to a ring of Aprica shapes as on their Play Gym (see p. 170).

Knuddel Cutlery

Ulrike Bögel
WMF AG, Germany
www.wmf.de

Product designer Ulrike Bögel set up her own design studio in Bavaria in 1982 and works in glass, porcelain, ceramics and metal. Some of her earlier cutlery designs are used by Lufthansa airlines. For her children's range, which she developed for the well-known German cutlery manufacturer WMF, she created these reduced, thicker shapes that are easy to grasp and manipulate. Made of metal rather than plastic, they have a certain solidity and sense of longevity about them as well holding their own appeal as design objects.

Splash, Chow

Scott Henderson
SKIP*HOP, USA
www.skiphop.com

Adding to the collection started by Ellen and Michael Diamant, designer and father-of-two Scott Henderson addresses the problems of early feeding, or the storage problems associated with it. The Splash is not just a drainer for baby bottles, it is a bright, sculptural addition to a kitchen all-too-easily cluttered with gear. The centre holds a rubber-gripped bottle brush and bottom shelf for teats, valves, caps, etc. and the whole rotates. Use for up to nine bottles or cups.

The Chow baby-food organizer can be used on the worktop, or counter, or in the cupboard, using two levels or three. Each level rotates separately, features a padded, non-slip base and can hold up to twelve jars. Splash and Chow are both available in blue, white or red.

Battery Square & Six of One ... Tableware

Keith Stephenson, Mark Hampshire
Absolute Zero Degrees, UK
www.minimoderns.com

Keith Stephenson and Mark Hampshire were working with their cutting-edge branding and design studio when they decided to apply some of their creative energy to homewares and then to children's products. They started with wallpaper 'because friends with children complained that there was no choice in interior products for them.' The original designs for the wallpaper (see p. 139) were so successful that the designers applied them to decorative tableware. The crockery is bone china with hand-applied decoration in delicate patterns and soft hues.

Dombo Cup

Richard Hutten
Richard Hutten Studio, Netherlands
www.richardhutten.com

Functional and fun for children, another innovative idea from designer Richard Hutten (see also p. 128) whose creations are in demand around the world. The Dombo is a cup that can be grasped and held steadily even by very young children. Oversized handles and a one-piece rotation-moulded form make it easy to hold and clean. It is also very durable, dishwasher safe, and comes in a variety of colours.

Robot & Monster Tableware

Jackie Shapiro
French Bull, USA
www.frenchbull.com

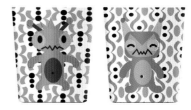

Designer Jackie Shapiro had a fine pedigree in designing for kids long before she came to set up her own brand. Working for Mattel, she helped create the Barbie and My Scene Style Guides as well as working on products based on characters from Cartoon Network. Her combinations of brilliant, appealing characters and quirky geometric patterning give her line of melamine plates, bowls and cups a slightly retro flavour that makes them attractive to parents and children. The tableware is high-heat resistant, dishwasher safe, shatterproof and made of durable materials that promise not to fade, discolour or chip.

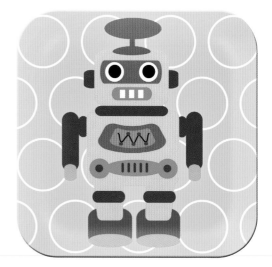

Rebel Children's Set

Johan Verde
Stelton A/S, Denmark
www.stelton.com

Norwegian designer Johan Verde's Rebel tableware is based on ergonomics and 'the particular way in which a small child grasps and moves, as well as the adults' need for elegant design'. The mug tapers outwards at the bottom to make it more stable on the surface. The spoon has a thick, curved stem for small hands to hold easily. The plate is actually a bowl within a bowl, so that food spilling over is caught in the concave edge. The plate and mug are made of porcelain, while the plate has a rubber bottom to hold it in place on the table. The spoon is made of stainless steel. 'The lines are continuous and have no closings,' explains Verde. 'They are meant to express a kind of confidence and harmony for both adult and child.'

Trebimbi Puppets Club Tableware

Rivadossi Sandro, Italy
www.rivadossi.it

Rivadossi Sandro are well-established makers of cutlery that feature handles in a variety of materials such as coloured, sculpted acrylic, wood and composites. But in 2000 they launched the product they seemed destined to deliver, the Trebimbi collection of children's tableware. The spoons, knives and forks all pose happy faces laser etched on stainless steel, while the polypropylene handles are formed in an array of jolly colours and easy-grip shape. All the designs click together to keep cutlery sorted and just for the fun of it. The Puppets Club range includes funnel-shaped figures and coordinated, mix-and-match plates, bowls and cups that all happily snap together too.

Baby Dinnerware

Nume, Italy
www.nume-design.it

The Nume approach to natural materials and fine, simple design which
they display in their furnishings (see pp. 94, 112, 156, 246) has lately
been applied to a new range of ceramic tableware for children. For
parents who cannot abide lots of plastic or just want to have something
to make meals special, Nume have created some lovable patterns on ivory
backgrounds that are pleasantly childish while adhering to the Nume
philosophy of 'pure forms'.

Snack Set

Not Neutral, USA
www.notneutral.com

Produced by the multi-disciplinary Los Angeles-based
design studio, Rios Clementi Hale, the Not Neutral
range of products for children is anything but bland
or confined to the character-driven precepts of story-
book design. Using bold graphic patterns and modern
hues, Not Neutral develop designs that are appealing
to children and their design-aware parents. The
Snack Sets made of sturdy melamine include a
practical set of vessels and cutlery including a wide,
square tray, plate and deep bowl that are easy for
small children to grip and use. They also make a
ceramic range in their Seasons and Transport
graphics (see p. 141).

Kipiis Bib Clip

Kipiis, USA
www.kipiis.com

The baby bib has undergone many transformations
in recent years. The standard terry tie-on has been
reworked in vinyl, given Velcro fasteners, had sleeves
added or a front pocket for catching dropped pieces
of food, and a number of other 'helpful' additions.
But the Kipiis (kipp-eez) Bib Clip is adaptation itself.
Clipping onto a napkin, kitchen towel or any bit of
cloth you might want to use, it makes a front
protector that can be washed, re-used or thrown away
but is unlikely to be yanked free. Available in four
colourways, Kipiis are upper-rack dishwasher safe.

Puzzle Tray

Wendy Boudewijns
Royal VKB, Netherlands
www.royalvkb.com

Wendy Boudewijns graduated from the Design Academy, Eindhoven, in 2005 and soon started her own studio, where she works on interiors, styling and design. She won the European Red Dot design award for this mealtime Puzzle Tray. The tray has non-slip feet, and the chunky melamine plate, cup and cutlery fit into cut-out spaces like a jigsaw. Like some board puzzles, the cutlery pieces have red grip pegs to make them easier to remove once in place.

Furniture

Junior Bedrooms, Tables & Chairs, Lounge Chairs

As much as children need furniture that can evolve, they also need robust design that can take hard use and still stand up, while continuing to look good. To do this some modern designers have taken a back-to-basics, craftsman-like approach, employing solid hardwood and durable, non-toxic, finishes with imaginative flair and, in many cases, handmade production. Others, including many of the European designers, achieve a combination of style and function using new materials and bright, distinctive forms that engage with a sense of play and adventure, whether for sleeping, sitting, creating or lolling about. Modular systems are regaining popularity as adequate storage is a vital part of a serene living space for children. While well-designed nursery furniture should be able to adapt from newborn to toddler use, the child's bedroom needs to cover a range from pre-school to junior, or even perhaps teenage years. Natural wood used for basic furnishings is not only environmentally preferable to many other materials, it is also supremely adaptable.

Many of the newest children's furnishings and objects reflect research into a child's development and learning stages. As modern parents strive to spend more time with their children, they become acutely aware of these advances in design. Those parents who might also be keen design enthusiasts want the furniture their children are using to reflect some of their own aesthetic leanings, a trend that today's designers have embraced beautifully.

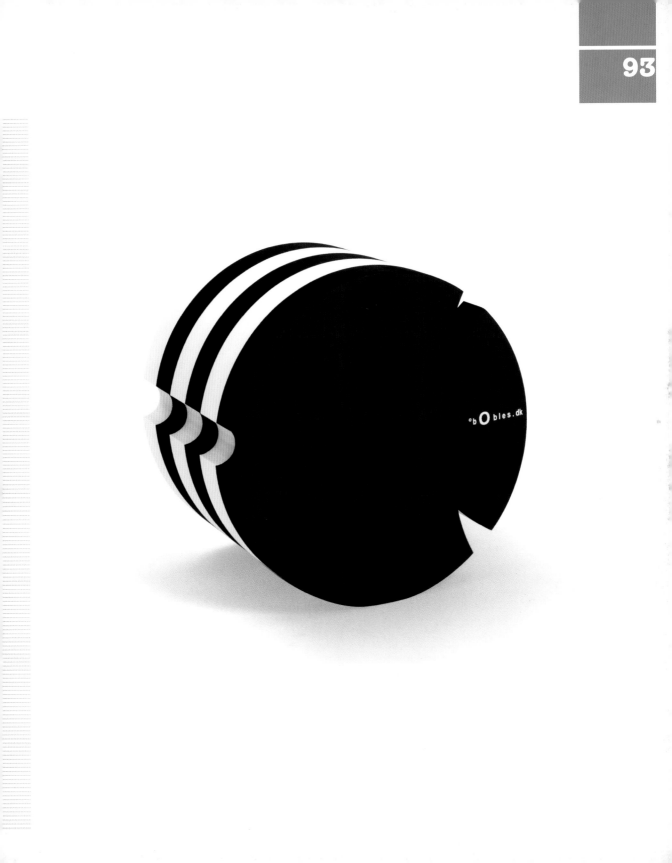

Bed 1 & 3

Nume, Italy
www.nume-design.it

Using their proven palette of birch plywood and natural fabrics in a range of good, basic colours combined with a flexible design, Nume have made a necessary piece of furniture into a little corner of fantasy. Bed 1, a modern-style canopy bed, is available in two sizes, as a single bed (daybed) or as a larger size that makes a great space for quiet play. Natural cotton fabric covers the sides and top. The mattress is pure English wool with sides in felt wool. Bed 3 is made of birch ply with fabric sides that can be removed when the child is old enough to get in and out on their own. Bed 3 is 156 cm (61 in.) long.

Platform Toddler/ Twin Bed

Kiersten Hathcock, Denise Love
Modmom, USA
www.modmomfurniture.com

Kiersten Hathcock is 'an ex-cable-tv marketing executive-turned-stay-at-home-mom-turned-self-taught furniture designer/builder'. Having learned woodworking from her carpenter father in his garage workshop, she says she 'rekindled her passion for woodworking' after leaving the corporate world. She now creates beautifully crafted wood furniture in her own garage workshop and is about to sell her products internationally. This ingenious birch bed converts from a toddler-safe smaller bed to a full-size twin by using guard rails that slot into the platform base.

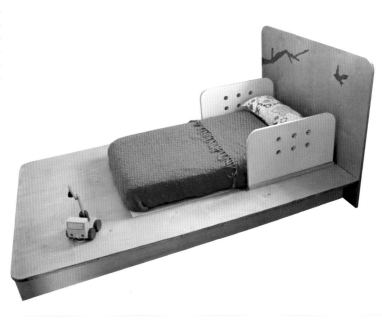

Skipper Bed

Loïck Peyron
Habitat, UK
www.habitat.net

World champion yachtsman Loïck Peyron was an inspired choice for someone to design a product for Habitat's VIP for Kids range. The bed recalls the compact space and efficiency, and the fabric and framework, of sailboat design to create a bed that is both functional and wonderfully imaginative. Peyron says he wanted to 'pack together' some of his dreams as a young boy in the design, 'like climbing to the top of Robinson Crusoe's hill; or looking at the stars through the window of my rocket.'

Petra Toddler Bed

Jenny Argie, Andrew Thornton
Argington, USA
www.argington.com

This toddler bed is a fine piece of woodworking. Like much of Argington's catalogue, its elegant simplicity is reminiscent of Arts and Crafts design, with subtle details and flourishes that add character to the piece. This bed is intended for use from 18 months. Being low to the ground (20 cm/8 in.), and with detachable side rails in matching wood, the bed is safe for children who have outgrown the cot but are not yet ready for a 'big' bed. It is made of birch wood and is available in five different finishes.

Cube

ducduc
ducduc, USA
www.ducducnyc.com

The ducduc design team was busily adding to their highly acclaimed line in 2007 and one of the new members was the Cube. A modern take on the old American 'corner group' of the 1960s, the Cube combines sleeping, relaxing, storing, creating and entertainment all in one. (See also pp. 52, 58, 119.)

Sparrow

Oeuf, USA
www.oeufnyc.com

Sophie Demenge and Michael Ryan achieved popular
recognition with their Classic nursery furnishings
(p. 59) in pure forms and convertible construction
that transforms from baby to toddler room. They
have achieved a similar stylistic longevity with the
Sparrow collection (shown here with Twin bed).
The furniture is made of solid birch and a non-toxic
lacquer finish in grey, rose and white.

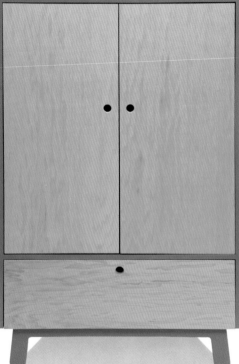

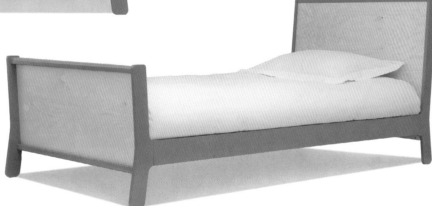

Uffizi Bunk Bed

Jenny Argie, Andrew Thornton
Argington, USA
www.argington.com

One of Argington's newest designs in their collection of artisanal wood furniture (see pp. 95, 114, 245), this is a modular, adaptable bunk bed with sophisticated lines and robust construction. The enclosed top bunk cantilevers slightly beyond the vertical support. The bottom platform bed, which sits low to the ground for younger children, can be parallel or perpendicular, or omitted completely so that the underneath can be used as a desk area with loft bed above. It is made from sustainable hardwood and birch ply.

Duet Bunk Bed

TRUCK Product Architecture
Nurseryworks, USA
www.nurseryworks.net

The bunk bed as the essential space-saving piece of furniture goes one better with the Duet, another stylish collaboration between the team at Nurseryworks and TRUCK Product Architecture (see also Studio Crib, p. 59). The bed and units can be configured in various ways, including having two 'stacked' beds with a wall of cubicle shelving at one end or unstacked with the separate cubicle shelving unit. When stacked, the top units can be accessed from the upper bunk. The furniture is finished in a range of bold colours or natural catalpa wood.

Warber Collection

Kristien Pilat
Warber, Netherlands
www.warber.com

Kristien Pilat worked for his father's firm Pilat & Pilat before embarking on the Warber collection of children's furnishings in 2003. The pieces, which all have 'poetic Friesian names' such as Romte ('space, openness') and Koes ('sleep warm and cosy'), are made from solid wood - oak, walnut and elm - by traditional craftsmen. The beds, wardrobes, cots and chests of drawers, while very hardy, are also just a bit fanciful. All pieces can be customized and all are finished with natural soap and oil. The cot converts to a child's bed or seat.

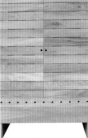

BB2 Collection

Julie Smith-Clementi, Frank Clementi
notNeutral, USA
www.notneutral.com

The Rios Clementi Hale studios home furnishings line notNeutral brings natural wood to children's bedroom furniture as well as gently curved forms. The BB2 collection includes boxed platform bed with footboard shelf/seat, side table, book shelf, mini rocker and mobile toy caddy made from environmentally friendly blonde birch Euro-ply. The pure, graceful forms make very adaptable arrangements, especially with graphic notNeutral rugs and wall stickers (see pp. 165, 141).

Furniture System

Suzanne Herbert, James Herbert
sixeight, Germany
www.sixeight.de

Architect-designers Suzanne and James Herbert met while studying at the Southern California Institute of Architecture and later set up their architectural practice in Düsseldorf, Germany, before conceiving the idea of a line of children's furnishings inspired by 'the functional aesthetic of the Bauhaus'. The modular plywood system is finely detailed and comes in either natural or coloured finishes. A range of components includes nursery pieces, such as the changing table, as well as desk, storage and loft/bunk arrangements. All units are made from Baltic birch plywood sourced from certified sustainably managed forests.

Kip Bed, Perf Boxes,
BroSis Chair, Look-Me Chair
Woody Chalkboard Table

Eric Pfeiffer
Pfeifferlab, Offi, USA
www.offi.com
www.pfeifferlab.com

Eric Pfeiffer spent years as a design director at the furniture design and manufacturing company Offi before setting out to create his own line of furnishings for adults and children. His bent ply tables, chairs and benches, as well as a range of modular seating and storage units, and delightfully simple bedroom furniture, have attracted admirers around the globe. His Kip Bed is a robust, modern unit that has friendly curved lines. Perf Boxes are funky, functional and fun to use, making sorting out kids' stuff something like child's play. The BroSis Chair attempts to bring a bit of sibling and design harmony. Look-Me chairs of birch ply are sturdy and lightweight mini design delicacies that are easy to carry and move, even for little hands. The circular Woody Chalkboard Table features a blackboard surface and useful central storage bucket.

Paola Antonelli
Curator

Paola Antonelli is Curator of Architecture and Design for The Museum of Modern Art, New York. A trained architect, she was a contributing editor for <u>Domus</u> magazine, has curated numerous highly acclaimed design exhibitions and was voted one of the one hundred most influential people in the world of art by <u>Art Review</u>. She is a lecturer at the Graduate School of Design at Harvard University.

'Design should be functional, indeed, but function is 1) not enough, 2) not everything, and 3) much more than just "working well".'

Going back to Munari, the Eameses and perhaps further back, many designers have created objects and furniture for kids. For some it has even been an integral part of their design process. Is this still true today? If not, what could designers today learn from these practices?
Many designers design for kids – and I am sure that you are familiar with them all. I do not believe that, taken as a group, they have something in particular to teach all other designers, and I do not think that other designers have something to learn from them a priori. There are good designers and bad designers, and the bad ones should learn from the good ones.

In an age of instant digital gratification, what do you think is the most important consideration in designing for kids today?
To be able to design really for kids, and not for adults in miniature or caricatures of the idea of kids. Design for kids is also a form of training. A designer should not give in completely to mass demand (just the same as for adults), but rather instil the idea of good design in children from when they are little. Children are amazing design critics. I have seen them in action many times, from when I was on the jury for the BBC Design Awards many moons ago – a bunch of us 'experts' picked the five finalists and then the BBC had a group of kids critique our choices, and it was humbling – to every single show I conceive. (If children get it and like it, the rest of the public will; it is mathematical.) There is no need to give them ribbon and sparkles and Disney- or Barbie-fied stuff; they will appreciate good work.

Above middle. Permis de Construire by Matali Crasset.
Above. <u>SAFE: Design Takes on Risk</u> by Paola Antonelli.

If design is supposed to be largely functional, what is the function of play in design?

Design should be functional, indeed, but function is 1) not enough, 2) not everything, and 3) much more than just 'working well'. As a matter of fact, you can consider providing emotion, friendliness, and comfort, as well as types of functions, and objects that deliver them are indeed functional (remember Tamagotchi). And play is very important because, as science has taught us, it is an amazingly effective tool for any analysis/synthesis, and therefore the design process. Moreover, playfulness is a way for the object to find an immediate communication with the person that uses it. Munari used the same subtle playfulness whether he was designing for kids, adults, or making art. Examples today include Matali Crasset, Martí Guixé, Fulguro, and many others.

'And play is very important because, as science has taught us, it is an amazingly effective tool for any analysis/synthesis, and therefore the design process.'

In this growing field, do you think there are any neglected areas of research or products? If so, which?

Hard to say. When it comes to commercial products, there is almost too much; I would not know where to start. More furniture with better prices would be a good start. There are new companies working on it – and I loved a few years ago the IKEA double armchair for dad and son, with the son lifted up to dad's height. Do you remember it?

What for you is an iconic design for kids?

Here is where I feel that I have no right to say! I am an adult now (most of the time), it is so hard to forget it. I am going to serve you some design icons – Lego, Mari's animals puzzle, you name it – but it is really kids you should ask. I wish the movie Big could become reality for you to finish the book well.

Flip Table

Amanda Levete, Jan Kaplicky, Future Systems
Habitat, UK
www.habitat.net

Asked to contribute a design to British furniture retailer Habitat's VIP for Kids range, Amanda Levete and Jan Kaplicky of the innovative architecture firm Future Systems called on their celebrated design for the Selfridges department store in Birmingham, England. The surface of the building is covered in thousands of discs which the architects used as a starting point. 'Link them in threes, then bend them and you have Flip,' say the designers, 'a table to sit at, sit on and crawl under.' They then used the offcuts to make flipnfriends (see p. 199).

Trioli Chair

Eero Aarnio
Magis Me Too, Italy
www.magismetoo.com

Finnish designer Eero Aarnio has been creating instant classics for design-loving adults, ever since he came out with his space-age Ball Chair and hanging Bubble chair in the 1960s. With the Me Too collection he has contributed what is sure to be another one for the history books. The Trioli chair is a piece of indoor-outdoor furniture and fun. It is a simple tubular plastic form with a seat positioned towards one end so that one way up it is a low seat, turned over it is a higher seat, and on its side it is a hiding place. A handle on the curved side makes it easy to carry; the bright colours and curved edges make it easy to love.

3D Puzzle Furniture

Elin Basander Lundin
Basander Lundin, Sweden
www.basanderlundin.se
www.funktionalley.com

Swedish designer Elin Basander Lundin won a Young
Swedish Designer Award 2006/7 for her design of
Miss Flatchair, part of her collection of 3D Puzzle
Furniture that also includes a table and shelf.
Children appreciate the giant fit-together forms and
parents find it useful for its flat-pack and folding-
away utility. The furniture is made from MDF with
AKZO Nobel allergy-tested and child-approved colours.

Paper Chair

Charlotte Friis
Charlotte Friis, Denmark
www.charlottefriis.com

Bringing together form, function and almost endless
creativity, Charlotte Friis's Paper Chair is one giant
roll of paper that a child can sit on, draw or colour on,
unroll, and on and on. Rolls are 500 m (1640 ft) long
and 32 cm (12½ in.) wide, and both sides of the paper
can be used. So there is not much danger of reaching
the end. The chair uses standard printing paper.

Play Table, Klick Couch & Chair

Play Table: P'kolino with the Rhode Island School of Design
Klick Couch & Chair: P'kolino with Davide Cesca
P'kolino, USA
www.pkolino.com

This company creates a range of adaptable furniture for children using modular interchangeable components. The Play Table consists of a bent maple table with curved end that can be repositioned as a ramp or 'lounge', and soft foam benches and stool components. It can take numerous colourful forms and is accessorized with the Lounge Pad that makes a comfortable lounge or tumbling mat. The Klick is a space-saving chair and table combination that fit together in a satisfying puzzle-lock, suitable for ages 3 to 7. The Couch and Chair are made up of birch ply units that can be used as seat frames or tables, with curved seat and rectangular ottoman cushions covered in soft suede microfibre fabric.

Funktion Object

Rosario Hurtado, Roberto Feo
El Ultimo Grito, UK
www.elultimogrito.co.uk

Industrial designer Rosario Hurtado and furniture designer Roberto Feo founded their design practice, El Ultimo Grito, in 1997 and soon won awards and wide coverage for their innovative products and furnishings. The Funktion Object is indicative of their desire to appeal to children and adults alike. The K-shaped pieces are made of rotational-moulded polyethylene and can work as a stool or in groups as 'design solutions', such as bases for tables or stacked shelving.

Ladrillos Shelves

Javier Mariscal
Magis Me Too, Italy
www.magismetoo.com

The Me Too collection has come up with yet another wonderfully creative toy-like utility piece in the Ladrillos shelving system by Javier Mariscal. Like his Nido (see p. 191), it utilizes brightly coloured plastic and undefined animal-like forms to appeal to growing minds and wide imaginations. Here he has put the animals to work holding up shelves made of smooth, white laminate. The colourful supports come in a choice of eight colours and character shapes and in two different heights (25 cm/10 in. or 35 cm/14 in.) to provide enough variation for the most vivid room scheme. Each shelf has a centre seam along which the supports can be positioned as needed and locked into place using specially designed fasteners.

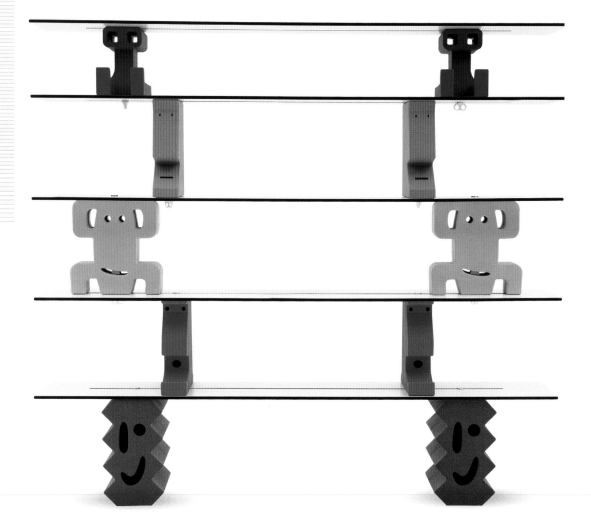

Romping Animals

Louise Blaedel, Bolette Blaedel
Bobles, Denmark
www.bobles.dk

Based on simple geometrical shapes and made from firm foam, these stylized animal forms encourage children to touch, roll, climb, sit and play. Their arresting, colourful forms are the result of a collaboration between sisters Louise and Bolette Blaedel, who explain that the design 'takes children's motor function as its starting point, but it is just as important that the piece of furniture itself is beautiful'. The animal motif was inspired by a trip to the zoo when Bolette's young son became so excited by the animals that he saw, even though he was less than a year old. The design was then ten years in the making and the result are these soft, round-edged shapes that the sisters say 'appeal to the basic senses. You can sit at different heights, play ball, surf, roll, see-saw... '. You can even lie down.

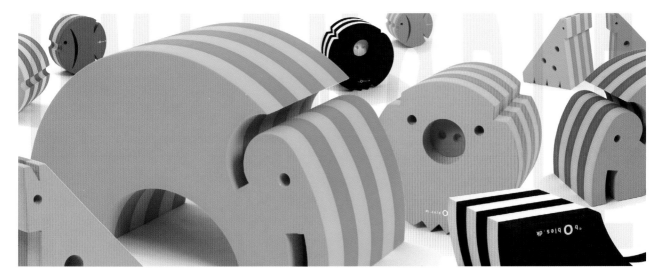

Roll-top Chair
& Bench

Simon Maidment
Offi, USA
www.offi.com

UK-based designer Simon Maidment took some of his inspiration from the old desk design that enabled you to conceal any desktop disarray by simply pulling a cover over it. The cover was a rather ingeniously conceived sheet of flexible wood traditionally made by gluing strips of shaped wood to a suede or fabric backing. Using the same device for a child's chair was, Maidment says, 'in response to a childhood memory. As a kid I never really understood the concept of clearing up. I thought that having all my toys in one pile was fine, even if that was in the centre of the room.' Now he hopes his chair design will provide other children 'somewhere special, perhaps even secretive, to store stuff'. Not only can they tidy their things away, but in Maidment's design the rolltop has been sturdily constructed so that they can sit on top of it, ensuring no one else gets their little hands on their treasures. Made of MDF with solid wood base, the chair is part of a range designed by Maidment for Offi and also includes a bench.

Sofa 1

Sabien Devriendt, Elisa Ossino
Nume, Italy
www.nume-design.it

Created in 2003, Nume combines the creative talents of Sabien Devriendt and Elisa Ossino, with the marketing expertise of Raffaella Ossino and Gabriele Troilo. Their vision is to produce furnishings and textiles that engage with a child through 'sensorial experience.' They do this using natural materials such as multilayer birch for framing, sheepskin, hand-woven wicker, felt, wool, pure linens and cottons. 'Turning back to the work of artisans and hand-crafted objects is a way of providing added value,' they say of their work. The modular sofa can also be used as building blocks, or made into a child-size guest bed. Upholstered in washable pure cotton, linen or wool in a range of colours, it combines modular style and convenience with kid-friendly durability.

Nume Table & Stool

Sabien Devriendt, Elisa Ossino
Nume, Italy
www.nume-design.it

The pairing of colourful details with a striking overall simplicity are a hallmark of Nume design. This children's Table and Stool, made of natural hardwood with coloured panels, is an elegant aid to the budding scholar at home.

Grace Table & Stools

Jennifer DeLonge
Jennifer Delonge, USA
www.jenniferdelonge.com

A self-starting entrepreneur, Jennifer DeLonge launched her own interior design firm before she had finished her undergraduate degree. After marrying rock musician Tom DeLonge and having her first child, she decided to try her hand at children's furnishings, with quick success. Her Grace Table and Stools have a pleasant chunky shape and bright polished appearance, but their simple forms make them suitable for grown-up rooms. Made of formaldehyde-free MDF and low VOC paint, they are available in five colours.

Fundy Play Table, Eiffel Bookcase

Jenny Argie, Andrew Thornton
Argington, USA
www.argington.com

Designers Jenny Argie and Andrew Thornton studied fine art and architecture before they had children and decided to start up their own children's furniture company. Their mission is to create pieces 'that are uniquely crafted with expertise in traditional woodworking techniques; that is, to rely on wood-to-wood joinery rather than using an excessive amount of screws and fasteners.' They were also concerned about 'quality, longevity and use of materials' as well as environmental impact. For these reasons they stick mainly to wood and only wood that comes from managed forests. They produce inventive and practical pieces like the Fundy Play Table, the Petra toddler bed (see p. 95) and the Eiffel Bookcase. The table is made of birch wood and lacquered MDF, with either dry erase or chalkboard top. The top opens on two sides, using slow-closing safety hinges, to reveal partitioned storage beneath. A drawer in the side provides extra storage for pens and crayons. Stainless steel legs with locking casters are provided in two heights, for tabletop use or for floor play.

The Eiffel Bookcase is an aesthetic gift for all parents struggling with the problem of storage in children's rooms. Featuring four cube and two shelf cupboards, as well as open shelving in the centre and on top of the bookcase, the Eiffel is also a tribute to the warm, sturdy and pleasing properties of wood. The surfaces show natural wood grain, and handles are cut away from the doors instead of added to the door; this provides a safe grip for little hands and a lovely smooth surface.

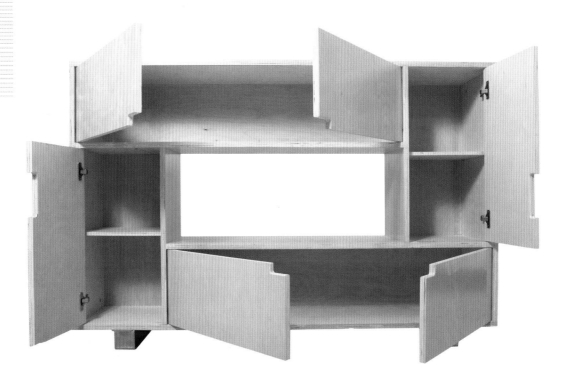

'A' Chair, 'A' Table

Frederic Collette
Collect Furniture, Denmark
www.collectfurniture.dk

Frederic Collette was educated in Civil Engineering
and has a Ph.D in bridge dynamics, but when his two
children arrived, his furniture-designing hobby turned
into a vocation. He founded Collect Furniture in 2007
and brought out his first designs in early 2008. His
inspiration comes from a desire to make children's
furniture that is suitable for design-savvy grown-up
spaces. His 'A' Table and Chair are designed on
inclined angles and have a certain graphic appeal.
Both have flush-fitted drawers with cut-out handles.
They are available in natural ply or painted finish.

Gradino

Toshimitsu Sasaki
Sasaki Design International, Japan
www.sdii.jp

Another beautifully crafted range from the design
studio of the late Toshimitsu Sasaki who was inspired
by the handmade works of craftsmen in the village
where he grew up. The Gradino desk, chair, shelf and
drawer units are made with the same modern shapes
and tactile appeal as the Carota chair (see p. 77). The
adjustable units are solid beech.

Panton Junior

Verner Panton
Vitra, Switzerland
www.vitra.com

Soon after Verner Panton first introduced his sculptural chair made of injection-moulded plastic with Vitra in 1960, he had the idea of producing a child's version. Sadly it never happened, despite the fact that children were immediately drawn to its bright hues and the smooth curving shape that give it the appeal of a child's plaything, while it still functions as a comfortable, sturdy piece of furniture. Several years later Vitra has found a way around financial obstacles to produce the Junior edition. It is 25 per cent smaller than the adult chair, but otherwise identical in shape and material. Available in seven modern colours, it is the junior design icon that has been waiting to happen.

Eames Chair & Stool

Charles Eames, Ray Eames
Vitra, Switzerland
www.vitra.com

Anyone concerned with 20th-century design has been touched by an Eames in one way or another, so why not the children of the 21st century? While many of Charles and Ray Eames' designs for Vitra could be described as playful, these bentwood objects are begging to be sat upon, held, carried, or stood upon by a child, who might one day grow up to do something even more fun.

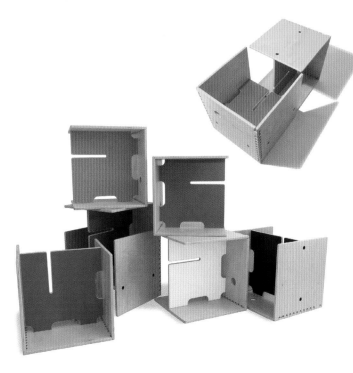

Max in the Box

Thomas Maitz
Perludi, Austria
www.perludi.com

This clever cubic creation in ply by Austrian designer Thomas Maitz has become an instant hit. It is functional, fun, compact, portable and adapatable. The simple wood box is fitted with a brightly coloured slat seat, with an off-centre notch that allow boxes to slide together to make a seat-and-desk arrangement or they may be stacked for shelving/seat/desk combinations. Maitz has also produced designs for a child's workbench and loftbed.

Mod Rocker, Mod Topper

Lisa Albin
Iglooplay, USA
www.iglooplay.com

Lisa Albin has an architecture and interiors studio in Brooklyn and was inspired to design the Mod Rocker and its table companion, the Mod Topper, by watching her children play and 'artfully create a sense of place'. In these and other furniture designs (see p. 126), Albin emphasizes sculptural forms, material variation and rich colours. She creates low organic shapes with wide proportions to facilitate ease of use. Made from moulded ply, with hardwood veneer and hard maple face with natural finish or cherry stain, the Mod Rocker has won American design awards and is sold by the MoMA store in New York.

Kids Rock

Alexander Taylor
Thorsten van Elten, UK
www.thorstenvanelten.com

Made of bent oak with rubber inlay, this children's
rocker is as modern and elegant as anything you
would want as an adult. It is by young British designer
Alexander Taylor who was voted Elle Designer of the
Year in 2005. His Fold lamp was acquired by the
Museum of Modern Art, New York, in 2006.

Austin Desk, Chair & Storage Unit

ducduc
ducduc, USA
www.ducducnyc.com

Part of the Austin range by ducduc, which includes a
full nursery collection, as well as a loft-bed/bunk and
sideboard, or credenza, the desk unit shares the
Austin aesthetic of limed-oak and painted hardwood.
The desk and chair reflect the ducduc credo of
'sustainable style'. All joints are lock-mitred for
strength. The desk is available in two heights with
optional entertainment system and computer/MP3-
player connectivity. The storage unit accommodates a
CPU. The desk chair has adjustable height, swivel and
castors and is made from hardwood. All the wood
comes from sustainable sources and all the products
are made by hand (see also pp. 52, 71, 96).

EVA Table,
Chair & Stool

Lawrence Tarantino,
Sharon Tarantino
Offi, USA
www.offi.com

Architect-designers Lawrence and
Sharon Tarantino opened their
architectural practice in 1984,
working on a range of public and
private buildings. In 2002 they
launched their Studio, offering
products such as children's
furnishings made from EVA foam,
the same durable and shock-
absorbing material used on the
soles of sneakers. The material
offers wide possibilities of appealing
colour combinations that make
simple, pleasing and safe designs
for toddlers and older children.

Benz Table

Ruth Kenan
Green Lullaby, Israel
www.green-lullaby.com

Ruth Kenan's discovery of the
stable and lightweight possibilities
of cardboard (see p. 44) led
obviously to other useful pieces.
She later developed a Bench (with
backrest), Table and Multi-box.
The Table has a removable top
and storage. Blank panels can be
decorated by parents or children.

Casakids
Hide-n-Sit
Armchair,
Rockabye
Rocker &
Sled Desk

Roberto Gil
Offi, USA
www.offi.com

When Offi launched their children's range in 2003, Argentinian-born designer Roberto Gil was one of the first they signed up. Working with design group Casa Kids Collection, Gil produced Casakids, a line of nursery and children's furniture that all follow an aesthetic of clean lines, child-friendly curves and two-tone and natural-wood palette. Forms are also compact and very sturdy. The Hide-n-Sit Armchair, Rockabye Rocker and Sled Desk have seats that lift to provide storage. The furniture is in non-toxic-painted MDF and Baltic birch plywood.

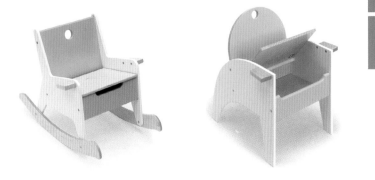

Mico

Rosario Hurtado, Roberto Feo (El Ultimo Grito)
Magis, Italy
www.magisdesign.com

The designers of El Ultimo Grito (see Funktion Object, p. 109) have had a successful collaboration with Italian manufacturer Magis, who have produced a highly acclaimed range of products for children. With Mico, Hurtado and Feo wanted to address the the period when children start to form their earliest memories with 'objects that could help them develop their own understanding of the world' through the exploration of physical forms. The Mico is designed to engage children as a functional plaything that will inspire creative associations and stories.

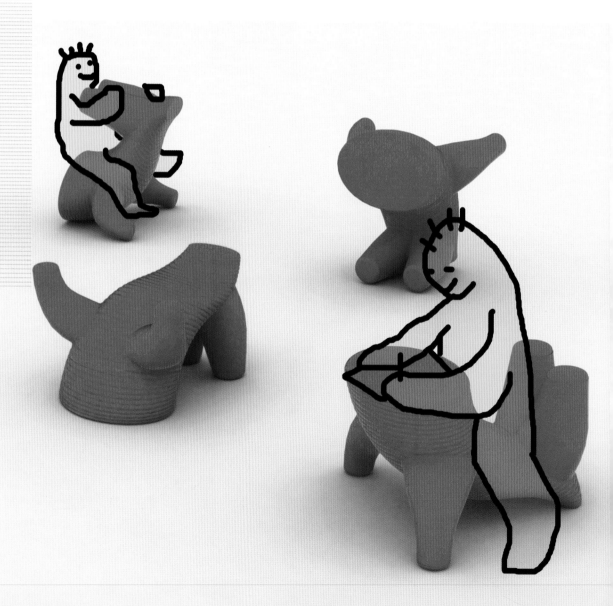

La forêt de boîtes

Matali Crasset
Balouga, France
www.Balouga.com

This child's desk in birch plywood is a 'forest' of little spaces to hide and display objects, photos and school supplies. Mother of two school-age children, Matali Crasset is a well-established designer who spent five years working for Philippe Starck before setting up her own studio. She has also created some wondrous large projects such as the interiors of the HI Hotel in Nice and the identity, website, interior and exterior design for SM's – Stedelijk Museum in s'-Hertogenbosch, the Netherlands. La forêt de boîtes is one of several innovative pieces she has developed for children (see p. 212).

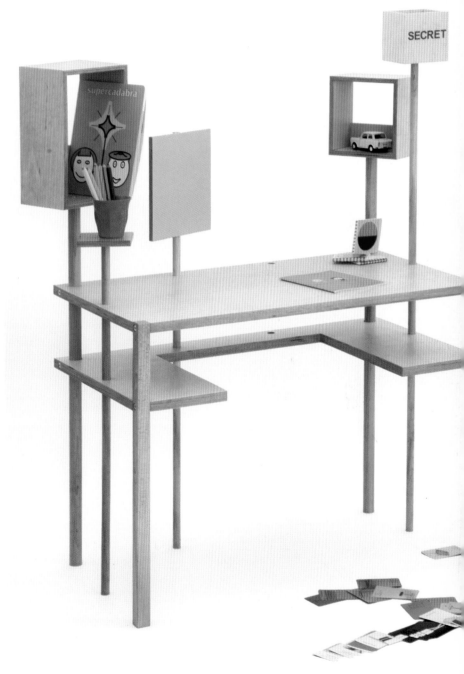

Hairy Bertoia Diamond Side Chair

Douglas Homer
DouglasHomer, USA
www.douglashomer.com

In his aim to 'reintroduce Harry Bertoia's work to a new generation of design enthusiasts', while also creating something 'a little more innovative, a little more unexpected ... to give the chair the "look at me" quality', Douglas Homer has certainly hit the mark. Starting out with an appreciation for Bertoia's Diamond Chair of the 1950s and the fact that 'there are huge numbers of these chairs that have seen better days' Homer developed a way to re-condition the metal structures of the adult- and child-size chairs while giving them 'an added squooshy-ness' by threading them with tubular neoprene strands shaped in the same diameter as the steel used in the chair. Each of the approximately 2500 strands are hand-knotted onto the sand-blasted, re-welded chair by Homer's 'assembly line' of stay-at-home mums located near his office in Lancaster, Pennsylvania, part of Homer's commitment to what he calls 'low-impact manufacturing.'

Pick Up

Alfredo Häberli
Offecct, Sweden
www.offecct.se

Argentine-born designer Alfredo Häberli studied industrial design in Zurich before going on to create for well-known brands throughout Europe such as Edra, Driade, Luceplan, Zanotta, Cappellini and Iittala. In 2002 he created the Pick Up chair after having seen the way his young son 'took his first steps and grabbed a stool to help him. I immediately saw what was needed'. The Pick Up is a 'combined chair, walking aid, travel and transport' vehicle. Even after Häberli's son could walk un-aided, he used the chair 'as a car loaded down with all his books.' Of course, the designer, says, 'when he has visitors, he takes them for a ride.'

Island, Point

Jukka Setala
Fatboy, Netherlands
www.fatboy.nl

The bean bag was re-made in 1998 by Finnish designer Jukka Setala into something altogether more modern, robust and appealing to all ages. The Fatboy label now presents everything from lounge furniture to pet beds. But the original squishy square Fatboy, the Island and the Point are perfectly bold, robust and great fun. Tough nylon fabric can be wiped clean.

Sono Kid

Dieter Paul
Dmp, Austria
www.dmp.co.at

Following on from Sigmund
Freud's ideas about shapes that
appeal to children, Austrian
designer Dieter Paul adapted the
design for his popular Sono chair
for adults to a smaller size and
more rounded form. Made of high-
quality foam and covered in soft
and elastic wipe-clean polyurethane,
the soft, L-shaped chair has an
additional ovoid nub that makes
a more springy seat, soft, safe and
fun to sit on. It is also available in
orange and blue for single orders.

Tea Pods

Lisa Albin
Iglooplay, USA
www.iglooplay.com

Lisa Albin, who won awards for her Mod Rocker
(see p. 118), designed the Tea Pods as 'sculptural and
movable furniture for children and adults'. The pieces
can be 'flipped' into different positions to become a
stool, a side table, bench, ottoman, lounger or just
a play object. Made of foam without internal wood
supports, they are safe to roll around on or with.
A tray can be fitted on top of the pods to create a
snack table. They are upholstered in ultrasuede with
a plush nap, wool or Crypton suede with anti-microbial
backing in a range of colours.

Min Chair

Chul Min Kang
industREALdesign, USA
www.minchair.com

As a group they resemble a scattering of sweets. The
Min Chair is a playful sculptural object as well as a
fun, colourful, stackable seat for children. Made from
a single piece of rotational moulded plastic, it can be
manufactured efficiently and is a sturdy piece of
furniture without any sharp corner or fittings. The
folded shape means it can be used as a seat or a
rocking horse-style plaything (and an added stopper
keeps the chair from tipping too far). A larger version
is available for adults.

Kapsule

Karim Rashid
Offi, USA
www.offi.com

One of the world's leading designers of products,
fashion, interiors, furniture and lighting, Egyptian-
born Karim Rashid started his own design firm in
New York in 1993. Though he has a vast catalogue
of products to his name, the Kapsule chair (2002)
for children has become something of an icon of
children's products. With its playful, bulbous contours,
candy colours and easy handling, it is a simple and
brilliant design. The cavity at the back functions as
a handle and open storage space.

Bronto Chair

Richard Hutten
Richard Hutten Studio, Netherlands
www.richardhutten.com

Both as a solo designer and as a member of the Droog collaborative Richard Hutten continues to create design objects that attract a worldwide following. In making the Bronto children's chair his aim was to make 'a constructionless piece of furniture'. To this end his studio developed their own rotation moulding machine that could work both hard and soft thermohardening material. In this way, the softer material ends up on the edges of the piece, so children cannot harm themselves, while a harder core makes the object strong enough to sit on. Every chair comes out differently in the process, making each a unique product. The Bronto is now in a number of museum collections, including London's Design Museum and the Stedelijk museum, Amsterdam.

Fat Cat

Christine Schwarzer, Anne Birgitte Balle
RoomMate, Denmark
www.roommate.dk

These bright, durable bean bags in abstract animal shapes were created by two friends who attended design school in Copenhagen together and decided to launch a line of children's products that were 'positive and stimulating' for children, but could also 'function as funny and charming design inputs to the grown-up environment'. The colours and shapes of their soft seats fit both criteria (as do their bags, p. 205 and Roomie dolls, p. 197). They also make flat versions of their bean bags called Pussy Cat and Big Bone for either children or pets.

Tiki Stool

Eric Pfeiffer
Offi, USA
www.offi.com

Eric Pfeiffer has become much better known for his natural, bentwood furniture (see p. 102), but this early design for Offi shows the range of his skill in exploring the possibilities of materials. Inspired by Tiki mugs and barware from the 1960s, the Tiki functions as a stool, bench or table. For children it is a delightfully undefined piece of furniture. It is made of rotationally moulded polypropylene and is available in six colours.

Pearl Chair

Christopher Robin Nordstrom
Our Children's Gorilla, Sweden
www.ourchildrensgorilla.com

Christopher Robin Nordstrom's quirky take on children's furnishings and accessories holds true to his idea that 'children's imagination is our inspiration' (also see pp. 192, 248). His Pearl Chair is part fantasy creature, part cartoon character, and is a sturdy little stool or chair. It is made of valcromat® an eco-friendly wood fibreboard.

Atollo, Dondolo, Tapeto Aprichiudo

ZPZ Partners (Atollo) RIGHT, Denis Santachiara (Dondolo)
RIGHT MIDDLE, Tullio Zini (Tappeto Aprichiduo) BELOW
Play+, Italy
www.playpiu.com

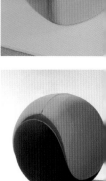

The line of soft furnishings manufactured by Play+ in
Italy is the result of an idea formulated by Maurizio
Fontanilli and created out of a collaboration between
the pedagogical consultancy Reggio Children with a
team of twenty-eight international designers working
under the art direction of ZPZ Partners. Each of the
250 pieces has an individual character formed by
a separate designer but all based on a body of
research into environments for children, 'and how
environmental stimuli affect child development and
interactions between children'. In particular the
researchers looked into 'soft qualities' such as tactility,
line and colour. (See also p. 193.)

Seesaw

Louise Campbell
Erik Jørgensen, Denmark
www.erik-joergensen.com

Designer Louise Campbell did not create the Seesaw
expressly for children but 'with clear references
to childhood'. As such, it has become one of those
products that started out as a playful approach to
adult furniture and became something that both
children and adults find irresistible. Setting out
to 'challenge normal expectations of upholstered
furniture', Campbell also crossed a line between
serious design and something altogether more
playful and inspiring. Described as 'equally suited
for brainstorming as for an informal chat', the
Seesaw also seems well suited to a bit of rocking,
climbing or just flopping about. Made of a steel
structure fully embedded in wood with polyurethane
cushioning covered in fabric.

Decoration & Textiles

**Mobiles, Wall Decoration, Sheets & Crib Bedding,
Blankets & Cushions, Rugs**

Decorating for the nursery was once all about pastels and
fairytales, but designs for children are now more practical
and better suited to what they respond to best. Studies
on early cognitive development have concluded that babies
under 6 months register high-contrast colours such as
black, white and red more profoundly than other tones
or hues. Patterns made from those colours are said to
give strong visual signals to the brain, resulting in a more
active, engaged response. As a result, toy manufacturers
concerned with infant development have marketed
playthings in high-contrast patterns. One of the most
obvious elements to be altered by the trend are hanging
mobiles, which have become early learning tools, and
simple, contrasting shapes and colours are now more the
norm than elaborate animal or character figures.

Wallpaper is coming back, but with bold new designs and
innovative cut-outs, and even paper that kids can help to
colour themselves (see p. 141). There is also a new trend
in removable vinyl wall stickers, enabling parents to
customize walls with a child's input in a non-permanent
way. In the USA, manufacturer BLIK has helped designers
create the ultimate in adaptable design with sticker
material that can be removed and used again without
leaving a mark. Children's bedding and textiles, too, are
produced in modern patterning and a sophisticated range
of colours. Characters and themes still feature, but in
much bolder styles and with coordinated prints.

Prize Hen, Click-A-Mobile Aeromobile, Locomobile & Sail Fun

Christian Flensted, Louise Helmersen
Flensted, Denmark
www.flensted-mobiles.com

A traditional craft in Denmark, mobiles have become a particular specialty of the Flensted family. Their business of creating modern mobiles began in 1954 when Christian Flensted and his wife, Grethe, created the Stork, which is an international favourite. Now working with a number of designers, Flensted make dozens of mobiles in wood, metal and plastic for adults and children. The colourful elephants might be their most recognized design, but their latest for children, the three-dimensional Click-A-Mobiles, are a wonderful addition to the collection. Their headquarters are suitably picturesque, located on the island of Funen in Denmark, where Hans Christian Andersen was born. The company occupies the old village school at Brenderup.

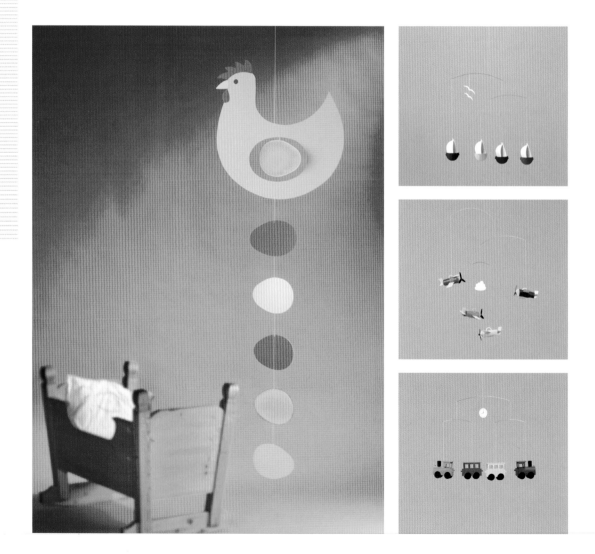

Wall Mobiles

Vilija Marshall
Oras Designs, USA
www.orasdesigns.com

Vilija Marshall's handmade mobiles have a very modern, yet slightly retro, flavour. Vilija makes two groups of mobiles - rectangles and ovals - cut in different sizes and forms with subtly contrasting colours. While they are not specifically intended for children, the growing demand for objects that aid children's development and nurture their early responses to contrast and pattern makes these delicate shapes well suited to the nursery. The dynamism of hanging shapes and shadows (part of the appeal, as they hang against the wall), demonstrate the skill for scenery design that Marshall developed while working in the USA and Italy creating environments for zoos, aquariums and theme parks as well as her experience in stop-motion animation.

Flash Card Mobile

Surya Sajnani
Wee Gallery, USA
www.weegallery.com

Designer Surya Sajnani turned her fascination with the idea that babies see high-contrast images best into a gallery of popular designs that take farm and zoo animals, and sea creatures, and turn them into dotty swirling masterpieces of child-friendly art for walls (see p. 140). The same characters are printed on 13 x 18 cm (5 x 7 in.) matte-laminated cards, which lend themselves to the construction of a jolly dynamic mobile using a Kikkerland or other photo mobile kit. Sajnani also reproduces her graphic creatures for stationery and wall canvases. The cards and the kit are available from Wee Gallery.

Mobile Rosy

Vilac, France
www.vilac.com

French toymakers Vilac have been turning out perfect little creations in painted wood since 1911. Set in the mountainous forest of Jura, Vilac credits the 'artisans of Moirans-en-Montagne' with the continued popularity over generations of the hundreds of figures that fill 'the world of Vilac'. Rosy the cow is a favourite personality and the simplified form, with black and white design and single coloured highlight looks very modern, though the company is nearly a century old.

Wallpaper Wildlife

Inke Heiland
Inke, Netherlands
www.inke.nl

Inke Heiland is a graduate of the Gerrit Rietveld Academy in Amsterdam and started her Wildlife designs as an idea for her own son's bedroom. She exhibited her first series of animal silhouettes cut from vintage and designer wallpapers in 2004. After an enthusiastic reception she expanded her range to include cut-outs of furniture and the 'Wallpaper Tree'. Because of the age of some of the wallpaper and the different printing techniques used, every cut-out is unique and the patterns are available in limited quantities. Animals include Elephant, Giraffe, Crocodile, Ostrich, Rhinoceros and Lion, as well as Tree and Birds. They are sold with paste and brush application kit.

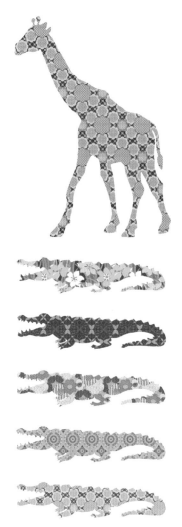

Tick-Tock, Knock-Knock, Battery Square & Six of One ... Wallpaper

Keith Stephenson, Mark Hampshire
Absolute Zero Degrees, UK
www.minimoderns.com

Keith Stephenson and Mark Hampshire of the London-based branding and design studio Absolute Zero Degrees started looking into the design of children's furnishings after complaints from friends about the dearth of good design. They started their children's range, Mini Moderns, with wallpaper. Avoiding 'imagery clichés', they produced four designs whose colours and shapes were inspired by 'Alexander Girard's Environmental Enrichment Panels for Herman Miller from the '60s and '70s and by vintage Galt Toys from the same period'. They are striking, for their rich, but subtle, tones and cleverly stylized, simplified forms.

Wee Gallery
Wall Graphics

Surya Sajnani
Wee Gallery, USA
www.weegallery.com

Taking her cue from parenting books that suggest the appeal of high-contrast images to babies, with their ability to see objects only a short distance away, artist and new mother Surya Sajnani created her first designs for what would become the Wee Gallery collection. Together, Sajnani and her husband, Dave, have now produced a range of items featuring her distinctive swirling black and white figures - elephants, giraffes, farm animals, sea creatures - on flash cards, mobiles, canvases and wall graphics. Made of vinyl, the removable and re-usable wall graphics are manufactured by BLIK (who also produce the notNeutral range, see p. 141) and are quick and easy to apply.

Wallpaper-By-Numbers

Jenny Wilkinson
Jenny Wilkinson Studio, UK
www.jennywilkinson.com

Soon after it was launched in 2003, Jenny Wilkinson's Wallpaper-By-Numbers range was deemed a design classic, with some pieces being acquired by the Victoria and Albert Museum, London, for their permanent collection. Though the initial designs were aimed at adults, the children's range quickly grabbed the attention of parents looking for a new approach to children's wall decoration. Themes include spacemen, tropical islands, fairies, hammerhead sharks and pirates. Hung like standard wallpaper, it can be coloured in using paints, coloured pencils or felt-tip pens.

Transport & Seasons Surface Graphics

notNeutral, USA
www.notneutral.com

NotNeutral is a home furnishings branch of Rios Clementi Hale, a multi-disciplinary design firm based in Los Angeles. Their striking graphics adorn a wide range of household accessories and their children's prints are particularly appealing. Using a clever blend of retro styling and sophisticated hues, the Transport and Season Surface Graphics make kids' rooms inviting and fun to be in even if you are grown up.

Dottilicious, CoCo's Caboose & Candy Factory Wall Stickers

Allison Krongard
WallCandy Arts, USA
www.wallcandyarts.com

The task of decorating children's rooms has become easier and much more fun since the advent of the removable wall sticker. Allison Krongard, founder of WallCandy Arts has made a fantastic contribution to the trend. After starting her career at Knoll International and coming from a family of modern furniture importers, Krongard hit on the idea of vinyl art to make 'stylish do-it-yourself environments on demand that can be installed, edited, adjusted, moved effortlessly without leaving any marks on the walls'. Offering both basic decorative shapes, such as the coloured spots of Dottilicious, as well as developed scenes such as Coco's Caboose and Candy Factory, Wall Candy is a bright versatile alternative to wallpaper, stencilling and other more labour-intensive treatments.

MagScapes

Patricia Adler
MagScapes, UK
www.magscapes.com

Designer Patricia Adler had already produced some
interactive interior concepts for the home, such as
her flat-pack acrylic chandelier and Qube modular
storage system when she hit on the idea of magnet-
receptive wallpaper. In addition to a range of coloured
wallpapers, Adler created themed sets of wall-magnet
decorations to use on them, such as frogs, coloured
discs, and MetroScape, featuring city landmarks and
iconic images in silhouette. MagScape wallpaper is
also now available in geometric, houndstooth and
1950s' retro designs.

Up in the Clouds
& Flyaway Stickers

Ben Reid, Simon Halfon
StickyUps, UK
www.stickyups.com

Graphic designers Ben Reid and Simon Halfon
worked in the fashion and music industries before
launching their line of removable wall stickers in
clever bold designs for children. Their sets of
butterflies, sheep, aeroplanes, stars, and cascading
numbers contain pieces in varied sizes of simple
shapes and colours that can be used to create
dynamic patterns or serene, subtle backdrops. Reid
and Halfon also design a range of wall stickers with
vegetal and geometric motifs for adult rooms.

Dino & Kevin wallpaper

Lotta Kvist
Sandberg, Sweden
www.sandbergtapeter.com

Swedish fabric manufacturers Sandberg pride them-selves on marrying high-quality contemporary design with traditional manufacturing techniques. Their in-house designers work closely with their production technicians and ink specialists in their own factory where their textiles and wallpapers are made. Sandberg have developed ranges specially designed for children with names like Dino, featuring dinosaurs, vegetation and other animals in line drawing, and Kevin, showing glossed abstract forms of helicopters against a matte background. Both were designed by Lotta Kvist for the Emma & Milton collection and come in several colours.

e-glue wall stickers

Marielle Baldelli, Sébastien Messerschmidt
e-glue, France
www.e-glue.fr

It is a wonderfully whacky world as illustrated by the creators of e-glue. French graphic designers Marielle Baldelli and Sébastien Messerschmidt design and handmake all of their products. With their e-glue wall stickers they hope to 'open a window of imagination by transforming walls into narrative spaces, where kids and parents can create, learn and have fun'. They have developed an extensive range of original characters and scenarios, all based on familiar themes but with a unique and often pleasantly weird twist. They also produce designs on commission.

Tom Dixon
Designer

A self-educated British designer who began his career making sculpture and furniture from scrap metal found around London and recycled materials, Tom Dixon quickly earned an international reputation. He was commissioned to design for Italian company Cappellini, for whom he created the S-Chair. In the 1990s he started working with plastics and created the iconic Jack light. Dixon has been Creative Director of furniture retailer Habitat since 2001, and in 2006 became Creative Director of the Finnish furniture company Artek. He founded his own design company, Tom Dixon, with David Begg in 2002.

'I think it beneficial to surround children with beautiful and functional things to use...'

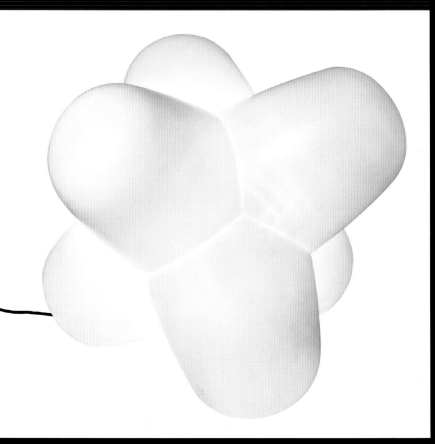

Above middle. Blow light
Above. The S-Chair
Right. Jack light

Is it possible – or necessary – to educate children about design?
**Not necessarily, although I think it beneficial to surround children
with beautiful and functional things to use.**

If design is supposed to be largely functional, what is the function
of play in design?
**I think a huge proportion of design currently is not even remotely
connected to functionality, but more concerned with style, profit,
product differentiation and play. The other side of the coin is that
play has a functional purpose.**

'A child is not a static thing.
What starts off as a pure being
is very rapidly tainted by
consumerism, not in decades
but in months.'

Given that a child's perception is much more 'pure' than that of
an adult jaded by decades of consumerism, is it possible for a child
to differentiate between 'design', 'experience' and 'emotion'?
**A child is not a static thing. What starts off as a pure being is very
rapidly tainted by consumerism , not in decades but in months.
Children also have very distinct levels of perception of experience
according to age and maturity.**

What product or existing piece of design would you most like to
redesign for children?
The urban street.

Great design produces 'childlike wonder' – what can designers learn
from the way kids see the world?
Naivety.

Scary Fish, Birdhouse, Lions, Tigers & Kitties ... Oh My!

Pixel Modern Pieces
Pixel, USA
www.pixelmodernpieces.com
www.pixelorganics.com

Making contemporary products that are still a bit whimsical is the aim of Los Angeles-based design team Pixel. They are also committed to producing their designs 'within our community' and to focusing on sustainability through reusable packaging and, in their Organics line, using organic cottons printed in with eco-friendly dyes and processing. What is most obvious about Pixel, however, is their slightly avant-garde approach to children's bedding. This is not grown-up designs for kids, but patterns and ideas that are lighthearted (and witty) while also being child- and style-friendly.

Elephant, Lion & Rocket Blankets, Pillow Landscape

Anja Grabenhorst
Apple Pie, Germany
www.apple-pie.eu

Interior designer Anja Grabenhorst spends most of her time creating sets for fairs and events and set-dressing for television. But as her mother was a tailor, Grabenhorst says 'I grew up with a sewing machine in my room and lots of fabrics.' Her attraction to fabrics helped her to create her exciting designs for children's blankets. She opted for the softness and durability of antipilling fleece to express her distinctive designs in appliqué, which is cut-out so that it is visible on both sides of the blanket. Working with contrasting colours and large forms that are visible even to small babies, Grabenhorst is also launching a new baby-sleeping bag that can be adapted to carriers and car seats.

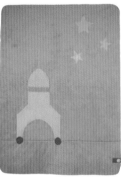

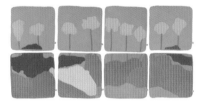

Cowboy & Carousel Kid Set

Christiane Lemieux, Jennifer Chused
Dwell, USA
www.dwellshop.com

After working as a fashion designer for Isaac Mizrahi and Gap, and as design director for a luxury home furnishings company, Christiane Lemieux founded Dwell, 'to bring modern textile design to the world of bedding'. Joined by creative partner Jennifer Chused (a magazine fashion stylist who also worked for Donna Karan and VH-1), the company brought out the brand Dwellbaby in 2002. Using a sophisticated design sense and a colour palette that is more subdued than many children's textile makers, they have produced a line of bedding for cots and children's rooms that have great appeal to modern parents. The designs are still fun and child-friendly, but without sacrificing a desire for style. The cowboy print, for example, is available in traditional pink or blue but uses gradations of colour and retro styling. Other prints use soft graphic patterns rather than cartoon shapes, in gently contrasting shades. The bedding is 100 per cent cotton percale.

Bamboo Fibre Bedding

Jane Powell, Kate Wakeman
Lotus Linens, Australia
www.lotuslinens.com.au

Using bamboo fibre is a recent practice among major textile producers but one that is set to grow as designers and manufacturers look for more efficient use of precious resources. When Jane Powell and Kate Wakeman set out to create clothing and bedding items for children that were 'elegant in their simplicity and doesn't brand them from birth' they did not yet know they would be on the cusp of a new development in natural fabrics. The pair initially thought to indulge their love of cotton but found that 'the environmental cost of growing cotton in Australia was just too high'. The 70:30 bamboo-cotton blend is both incredibly soft and naturally absorbent. Lotus apply simple, flowing graphics in subdued natural hues to make easy wash-and-wear fabrics available as cot blankets, sheets, child quilts, babygrows and pyjamas.

Pretty Square, What a Dish

Denyse Schmidt
Denyse Schmidt Quilts, USA
www.dsquilts.com/sh_baby

Located in a historic textile-producing region of the USA, Denyse Schmidt Quilts have been making traditional-style quilts for over a decade. Schmidt is a thorough devotee of quilt-making, giving classes, tours of her studio and selling her own-design fabrics and 'scrap bags' for creative quilting at home. A graduate of the Rhode Island School of Design, she combines a modern sense of colour and pattern with a renewed appreciation for a much-loved American icon, the patchwork quilt. The Baby set includes crib quilt, buffer or bumper, and pillow cover or sham. The Baby line is produced in partnership with the female-owned Sarita Handa Exports manufacturing company where the pieces are handcrafted in India.

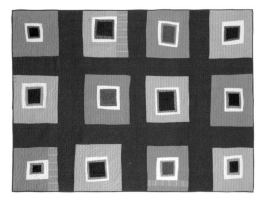

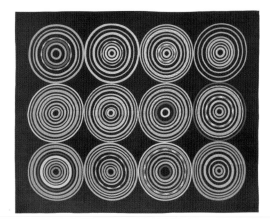

Gus & Max Collection

Mari Jansdotter
Gustav Maxwell & Co, USA
www.gustavmaxwell.com

Gustav Maxwell is the creation of Mari Jansdotter who had no formal design training before setting up shop in 2003, but 'a keen interest in modern interiors and design and in providing modern products to parents'. Her product line consists of crib-to-toddler sets including crib buffer, or bumper, reversible bedskirt, quilts and fitted sheets, as well as bedding specially designed to fit Stokke cribs and beds (see p. 54). True to Jansdotter's aims the Gus & Max Collection is made up of modern patterns and colour combinations (in cotton, 220 thread count) that are still appealing to children. There are also blankets and accessories in their own Ultra Soft fabric, a washable polychenille (see p. 133) that holds its softness so well through washings that Jansdotter uses it on a changing pad.

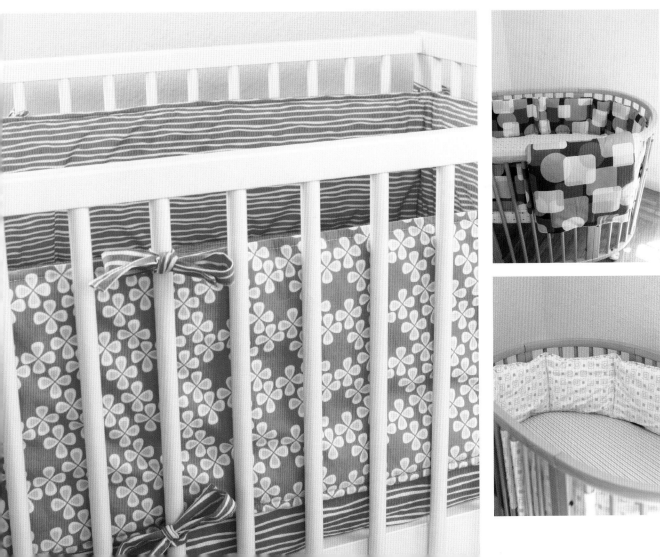

Saga fabric

Hanna Wendelbo-Hansson, Anna Sundberg
Sandberg, Sweden
www.sandbergtapeter.com

Part of the Kaspar & Saga fabric line from Sandberg,
Saga is a whimsical, colourful townscape with lollipop
trees and oversized daisies. Buildings covered in
stripes and swirls are playful too, but with architectural
definition and elements that make them much more
appealing than mere childish fantasy.

Elliot & Sebastian fabric

Hans-Jörgen Hansson
Egget Design, Sweden
www.egget.se

Hans-Jörgen Hansson studied art and graphic design in Stockholm and Malmo, and devised his Elliot and Sebastian patterns to bridge the gap between 'the super romantic language of the smallest kids' and the character preferences for 'Disney and Superman further up the ages'. Hansson says he is always looking for 'movement' in the patterns he creates. Elliot was inspired by his son.

Dozens O' Dots &
Town Square
Fabric Cushions

Keith Stephenson, Mark Hampshire
Absolute Zero Degrees, UK
www.minimoderns.com

Taking the patterns they created for their wallpaper
range (see p. 139) a step further, the designers of
the Mini Moderns range combined elements of their
wallpaper designs to create prints for fabrics. Battery
Square and Six of One... were combined to create
Dozens O' Dots; the number and building icons for
the Town and Knock Knock prints were brought
together to make the fabric Town Square. The fabric
is also sold by the metre and is available in cotton
and wipe-clean, plastic-coated cotton. Tablecloths and
napkins are also available.

Re-cover blanket

Tim Brauns, Hendrik Gackstatter, Fax Quintus
E27, Germany
www.e27.com

Swinging a child in a blanket may seem like one
of those activities banished to history, bearing in
mind our contemporary preoccupations with safety,
especially when it comes to children. But Tim Brauns,
Hendrik Gackstatter and Fax Quintus see things
differently. They say the Re-serve is a blanket 'to
lovingly rock' children in, but children may find other
more exciting uses for it. Made of 80 per cent wool, 20
per cent acrylic, it has four handles and has been tried
out on Quintus's son Moritz, now 6, who is 'our
encouraged test pilot and inspiration for further
products'. Gackstatter's son Jun-min, born in February
2007, has been drafted onto the testing team as well.

Thilde Pillow, Rag & Pocket

Pia Eriksson
Pia Eriksson Textilverkstad, Sweden
www.thilde.se

Swedish textile designer Pia Eriksson's idea to make a 'comfort pillow' and 'security rag' featuring an assortment of laundry labels in different sizes and colours was inspired by her daughter Thilde. Like many babies, Thilde was often more interested in playing with the small fabric tags attached to a soft toy or blanket than the object itself. The pillow and rag are made of colourful fabric patchwork designed by Eriksson with an array of labels attached for children to touch, twist, chew and hold onto. The Thilde pocket (not shown) was an unabashed attempt to get a bit more sleep in the morning. Its many pockets of various sizes are designed to hold enough toys and pet objects to keep an early-rising baby happy for at least several minutes.

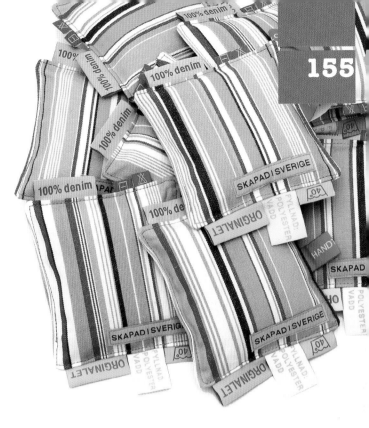

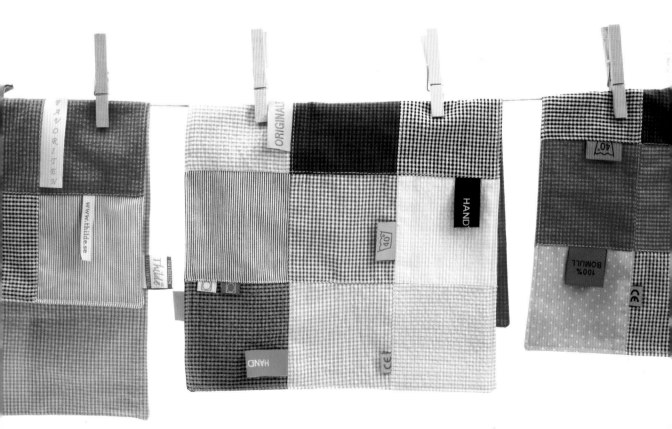

Nume Bedding & Pillows

Nume, Italy
www.nume-design.it

Using felt wool, linen, cotton and canvas in a mix of bold and neutral tones, these are choices for the subdued, sophisticated child's room. Their playful images and bold stitching make them undeniably child-friendly, however, and give an essential soft touch.

Space, Circus, World

Boodalee, USA
www.boodalee.com

Jeanice Skvaril was a mother of a young baby when
she decided there were no bedding options for the next
stage in her son's life that she could countenance.
'I had seen the enemy,' she says, 'licensed characters
commandeering children's bedrooms, crawling onto
their beds, stifling their imaginations.' Opposed to
'the mainstream commercial mediocrity offered by
big retailers', neither did she want her own 'minimalist
preferences' to dominate. So she gathered a team
of professionals to create the buoyant graphics of
Boodalee. Each themed set features bright iconic
figures and bold shapes in dynamic patterns. The
colours and details are sophisticated, but highly
engaging. For example, World features landmark
buildings against a riot of pattern. The fabric is
250 thread count, 100 per cent cotton.

Koeka
Sleeping Bag
& Playpen
Blanket

Margaret de Haas
Koeka, Netherlands
www.koeka.com

Greater awareness of chemical
dyes used in the manufacturing
process, sustainable resources and
childhood allergies has given rise
to a demand for purity in fabrics
used for children. Margaret and
Richard de Haas answer all of
these demands as well as that for
bright and beautiful options in
soft, textured terry and waffle.

Butterfly Ballet,
Loop de Loop, Pinwheel

twenty2, Rosemary Hallgarten
Nurseryworks, USA
www.nurseryworks.net

Traci Fleming and Kaye Popofsky Kramer have collaborated with
designers for their Nurseryworks furnishings (see pp. 59, 99), and their
creations of bedding for the nursery and child's bedroom have been no
less fruitful. With design group twenty2 they have produced a range of
coordinated twin bedding that walks a line between playful and abstract.
Butterflies navigate a black trellis motif in a fuchsia, black and white
colourway. Navy, aqua and blue is the combination for Loop de Loop, a
flight of paper airplanes. Rosemary Hallgarten's Pinwheel designs for
the crib use a modern palette with cleverly coordinated sheets and
pillow cases. All the bedding is 100 per cent cotton poplin.

Cuadros

Nani Marquina
Nani Marquina, Spain
www.nanimarquina.com

Renowned for her wonderfully 'three-dimensional'
hand-loomed rugs such as Roses, like a thick field
of flowers on the living room floor, or Topissimo,
made of thousands of coloured baubles, Nani Marquina
naturally turned her imagination to rugs suited to
children. The Cuadros is a flat pile rug in red, navy
and violet, or in more subdued pale greens and blues.
The rugs are handmade and hand-tufted using a
'pistol-like device that fires and then cuts a portion
of the wool, inserting it into a cotton cloth base'.

Flying Carpet

Ana Mir, Emili Padrós
Nani Marquina, Spain
www.nanimarquina.com

Since having children requires spending so much time on the floor, it is fortunate that the innovative Spanish rug designer has turned her attention to rugs for children. Now contributing to the Nani Marquina line, Ana Mir and Emili Padrós both studied industrial design at London's Central St Martin's School of Art and Design before returning to Spain to set up their design studio Emiliana in Barcelona. The Flying Carpet combines the texture of a 100 per cent handloomed wool rug with sculptural raised corners that make a piece of floor furniture suited to sitting or reclining. It may not have been designed specifically for children, but like many great products its appeal easily crosses all age groups.

Pillow Play

Ana Mir
Nani Marquina, Spain
www.nanimarquina.com

Kids will always play with pillows, and will always want to roll on them, jump on them and throw them. Large pillows, small pillows, any pillows, do not need to be designed specially for children in order for children to have their way with them. However, these pillows, produced by high-end rug designer Nani Marquina, are designed to look fantastic and still withstand, or perhaps encourage, more active treatment than a stylish cocktail party. Made of 80 per cent polyamide and 20 per cent Lycra®Elastane with polystyrene expanded beads inside, they are washable, and according to the manufacturers, can also be used in water. At least they should survive the odd chocolate or jam smear then.

Puzzle Rugs, Cut-out Curtains

Lily Latifi
Lily Latifi, France
www.lilylatifi.com

Based in a vibrant artisan's quarter of Montmartre in Paris, Lily Latifi has a shop filled with her fantastic designs in cut-out felt and other wonderfully tactile materials. Her puzzle carpets of interlocking felt pieces are a joy to create with, and pleasure on the feet. Her range also includes puzzle stools of stabilized foam and teddy bear cut-out curtains.

Baby Zoo Rug, Good Night Lamp

Laurene Leon Boym
Boym, USA
www.boym.com

An established industrial designer with work displayed in a number of museums and a successful partnership with designer husband, Constantin Boym, Laurene Leon Boym became inspired by forms in nature from reading books to her young son. Working with a small rug workshop in New Jersey she came up with 'hieroglyphic patterns based on a series of fictional animals', which were also partly influenced by primitive drawings such as the cave paintings of Lascaux. With lighting company Flos, she developed a small circular rechargeable LED light that glows softly around the edges and makes a comforting night light. The lights became integrated into the design of the rugs and the project became 'a fusion of two cultures: technological and hand-crafted.' The graphic-patterned rugs feature a circle described for the separate glowing disk light with mirrored top. The rugs are made of 100 per cent wool and are coloured with vegetable dyes.

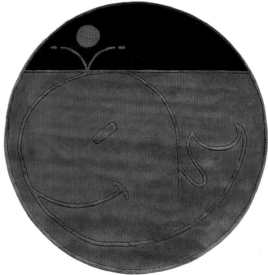

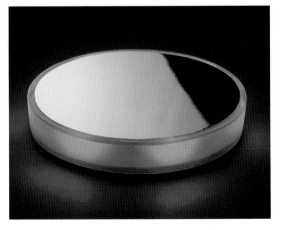

Puzzle Rug

Satyendra Pakhalé
Magis, Italy
www.magismetoo.com

Part of the playful Me Too range
by Magis (see also pp. 106, 110,
191), this puzzle carpet designed
by Satyendra Pakhalé is made of
soft expanded polyethylene and
polyester fabric formed into a
sturdy set of pieces for re-arranging
on the floor. The carpet is available
in grass, water or sand pattern.

Meadow, Town, Flower Hearts

HABA, Germany
www.haba.de

Formed by the merging of two companies in 1938,
German brand HABA describes itself as 'a wood
manufacturing company known for our high-quality
baby and children's toys'. More than that, HABA offers
a vast selection of furniture, toys, games and decorative
objects that range from the fanciful to the fundamental.
A number of HABA products demonstrate that their
designers can keep coming up with fresh ideas. The
HABA rug range features some fantastically vivid
designs that are both modern and fun. Meadow is wool
with a cloth backing (135 x 105 cm/53 x 41 in.).
Town is made of polyacrylic with a textile backing;
and Flower Hearts is 100 per cent New Zealand wool
on a textile backing (120 x 120 cm/47 x 47 in.).

Seasons

Julie Smith-Clementi, Frank Clementi
notNeutral, USA
www.notneutral.com

Julie Smith-Clementi and Frank Clementi of the Rios Clementi Hale Studios in Los Angeles are responsible for the children's furnishings, tableware and decorative designs of the collaborative notNeutral (see pp. 90, 100, 141). The same graphic patterns they developed for a range of whimsical wall stickers (produced by BLIK, p. 141) are used in stylish rug patterns for bedrooms or playrooms. 100 per cent wool rugs come in Links, Transport and Seasons motifs, and two sizes.

Smarties

The Rug Company, UK
www.therugcompany.info

Leading designer/maker of handmade rugs, The Rug
Company has a popular following among interior
designers whom it serves through three main stores
in London, New York and Los Angeles. Their own
design for a child and parent-friendly rug features
graphic images of a beloved British sweet strewn
across a neutral background. The rug is made of
hand-knotted Tibetan wool and measures approximately
274 x 183 cm (108 x 72 in.).

Candy Flower

Marni
The Rug Company, UK
www.therugcompany.info

The team at fashion design studio Marni created this
pretty floral pattern for The Rug Company's exclusive
collection. It was not intended as a children's rug, but
it has become a popular choice for girls' bedrooms.
It is hand-knotted Tibetan wool and measures
approximately 274 x 183 cm (108 x 72 in.).

Ark

Paul Smith
The Rug Company, UK
www.therugcompany.info

Paul Smith has joined the ranks of all-star designers who have contributed designs to The Rug Company line. This wallhanging depicts the story of Noah's Ark, with stylized paired animals and a smiling boat, all of whom look to be having a heavenly time. The rug is hand-stitched wool needlepoint and measures 172 x 112 cm (68 x 44 in.).

Toys

**Play & Objects, Building Blocks, Things That Go, Ride-ons
& Trolleys, Play Houses, Dolls' Houses, Dolls, Creative**

Late 20th-century research into child development has
resulted in innovations in children's products. Many new
'toys' designed for babies are more tactile, satisfying to
hold and easy to grasp. As children begin to really play,
they are now greeted with toys designed to stimulate or
to encourage fine motor skills and hand–eye coordination,
and to engage with their natural attraction to colour and
texture. That children appreciate the texture of cloth or
wood over hard plastic is something that is taking longer
to percolate through toy manufacturers, but it is coming
through independent designers.

Part of the move towards innovation in toy design must
be down to a generation of parents determined to spend
more time interacting with their children, which means
they are more aware of their children's environments and
the things that amuse and interest them. For the educated
parent, toys, whether they are dolls or computer games,
can all be learning tools, albeit fun, rather than just
sources of entertainment. And many parents expect to be
entertained or at least somewhat intrigued with the toys
that their children play with, even though most accept
that there will always be some objects, such as certain
branded characters, that children will become enamoured
of, but which will never serve any real developmental
purpose for the child or have any aesthetic appeal for the
design-conscious adult.

Play Gym

Aprica, Italy
www.aprica-italia.it

Play gyms are wonderful things, but usually only
required for a short period. While some convert to
toddler toys, this rather simple contraption converts
to a stand that can hold magazines (or books) or, by
taking out one of the top posts and adding a fabric
seat, a rather lovely toddler chair. Featuring colourful,
soft-formed creatures, 'the seven knights of love' are
meant to protect babies as they sleep and play.

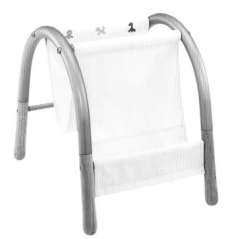

Skwish

Pappa Geppetto's Toy Company
Manhattan Toy, USA
www.manhattantoy.com

When Buckminster Fuller coined the term 'tensegrity' to describe a closed structural system of elongate compression struts within a network of tension tendons, he could not have envisioned the rise of the Skwish as the must-have baby toy of the 1990s. Originally produced by Pappa Geppetto's Toy Company in 1988, the composition of coloured wood in bright non-toxic colours and elastic bands has won numerous awards and a devout following among parents of babies and young children. Now produced by the Manhattan Toy Company, the Skwish is available in two colourways among their range of child development toys.

Stacrobats

Sandra Higashi, Byron Glaser
Zolo, USA
www.zolo.com

After studying at Art Center College of Design in Pasadena, California, Sandra Higashi and Byron Glaser founded their own multi-dimensional graphic design firm in New York and soon afterwards developed Zolo Toys. Their first designs for 'free-form, gender-neutral construction toys' were quickly recognized for their innovation and appeal (see p. 177). The Stacrobats are part of a soft-toy collection aimed at younger children than the Zolo construction kits. The soft fabric figures are fitted with magnetic appendages that help them stick and stack in frolicsome groups. With their vibrant colours and friendly features they are both dolls and creative construction toys.

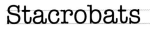

Bilibo

Alex Hochstrasser
Active People, Switzerland
www.bilibo.com

It is one of those toys that seems glaringly obvious in its appeal: a bowl-shaped piece of plastic in a range of bright colours. For anyone who has ever entertained children in the kitchen the plastic mixing bowls are always a hit. With Bilibo children have a basic object that really lets the imagination run wild. They can sit in it, spin around in it, carry toys in it, or, if there are more than one, stack them into a colourful tower. In fact the stacking aspect can be fully explored in the sibling toy, Bilibo Mini, and colour-combining Bilibo Pixel. Swiss designer Alex Hochstrasser launched Bilibo in 2001 and it has won an array of UK and European design awards, and is in several museum collections. It is constructed of 'virtually unbreakable' food-grade, high-density polyethylene and is completely recyclable.

Babal

Alex Hochstrasser
Active People, Switzerland
www.activepeople.com

Alex Hochstrasser is like a one-man toy-making
machine. After working for renowned design firms in
New York, Barcelona and Tokyo, he began his career
as a toy designer with the award-winning Bilibo (see
opposite). His design for the Astrojax, a dexterity toy
that involves spinning three soft balls on a string in
a way that keeps them constantly in motion and not
touching one another, inspired his move to Swiss toy
company Active People, for whom he created the
Babal balls. These are yet another bright contribution
to 'open-ended play' that allows children to explore
shapes and ideas without dictating goals. Made from
fantastically squishable elastic polyurethane foam,
the Babal and smaller 'junior' are a ball within a ball.
They can be fitted together or played with separately.
The balls have a flattened bottom so that they can
also be stacked into towers if you get more than one
set. They come in six colours.

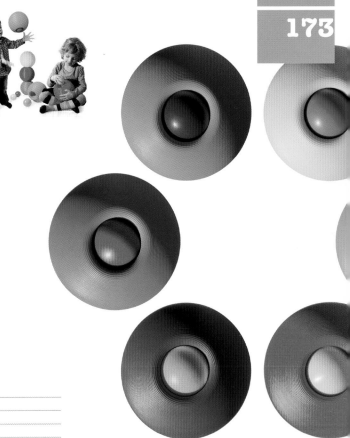

[YO]² Delta

Alex Hochstrasser, Lee Spector
Active People, Switzerland
www.activepeople.com

Another Alex Hochstrasser invention for children who like a little more
activity: a combination yo-yo and spinning top. The cone-shaped toy can
be worked up and down on its string like a yo-yo, but also spun on end
over a flat surface, adding a whole new dimension to the yo-yo fanatic's
bag of tricks. Like the Astrojax before it, the [YO]² Delta is sure to merit
its own YouTube stunts page.

Y-water

Yves Béhar
Fuseproject, USA
www.fuseproject.com

Designer Yves Béhar is known for taking unorthodox approaches to design challenges (see p. 76). His latest brainstorm combines children's love of drinks in fun containers and simple, but unusual, building blocks. The Y-water product is a plastic triangular-noded container that holds a healthy drink for children and can also be used as a toy by linking it with other empty containers to create colourful arrangements that seem to approach molecular structures – design is everywhere.

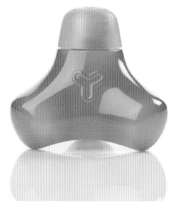

Cathedral Blocks,
Fantasy Blocks,
First Blocks

HABA, Germany
www.haba.de

It is not hard to see how HABA have maintained their pre-eminence as makers of wood furnishings and toys. Many of their building blocks, as here, continue to win design and play awards. Build a cathedral or a village with these lovely, chunky arching shapes. They are satisfying to stack together, as the shapes fit onto one another, and details such as the circular openings, peaked roofs and vibrant colours create imaginative building scenes. The Fantasy set has pieces in varied geometric shapes with extra coloured decoration that still offer opportunities for open-ended play in the endless variations. First Blocks (1+ years) have added dynamic elements such as beads or noisemakers or mirror panels, and a friendly character in his own little car.

Dado Cubes

Mark Carson
Fat Brain Toy Co., USA
www.fatbraintoyco.com

In 2006 graphic designer and businessman Mark Carson launched the Fat Brain Toy Company along with business partner John Batcher. Having looked closely at the toys his children were playing with, Carson started investigating what it was that made 'a really great toy', those that 'pull together imagination, creativity, wonder and delight'. Inspired in 2005 by the announcement that the cardboard box had been inducted into the American National Toy Hall of Fame, Carson hit on the idea of stacking boxes, or cubes. Soon the Dado Cubes were born along with his new company, which sells Carson's own designs as well as hundreds of carefully chosen toys that meet Carson's high demands and educational concepts. The Dado Cubes come in a set of ten colours slightly off the standard primary spectrum. They have won a string of awards and support visual-spatial learning.

Spaceframe Sculpture Kit

Scott Klinker
Offi & Company, USA
www.offi.com

'Most kids have more fun crawling into a cardboard box than playing with the toys we designers dream up,' says Scott Klinker of the inspiration behind his Spaceframe Sculpture Kit. The oversized pieces are notched to fit each other and create an array of large-scale (by kids' standards), three-dimensional shapes. 'Kids are naturally physical,' says Klinker. 'They like to build and inhabit a personal space like a fort and they like construction toys too, like Lego.' Klinker felt he found the ideal material (PET, a polyester fibre that is 100 per cent recyclable) to combine both those ideas. 'It's what I wished for as a kid,' he says. Each set includes twenty pieces in four different sizes.

Cuboro

Matthias Etter
Cuboro, Switzerland
www.cuboro.ch

Matthias Etter developed the first Cuboro as an
instructional game containing six basic elements
while working with school children in 1979. Etter,
now managing director of Cuboro, expanded the set
and launched the product in 1985. There are now
supplementary sets and eighty-two different
elements. Made of untreated beech from sustainable
cultivated forests, the blocks can be constructed in
endless variations and have earned numerous
awards and spawned as many competitions for
assembling the largest or most innovative
constructions. At home they offer opportunities for
exploring geometry, pattern and flow, and for the
satisfying clatter of racing marbles.

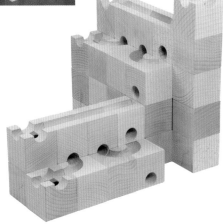

Geomag, Baby Magic Attractions

Claudio Vincentelli
Geomag SA, Switzerland
www.geomagsa.com

Italian inventor Claudio Vincentelli was reportedly
looking for magnetic bricks to subsitute for a more
traditional interlocking building system when he
discovered the original Geomag concept of magnetic
rods and nickel spheres. The system evolved to
include the coloured transparent plastic panels which
combine to make pyramid or box structures, and the
DekoPanels, which can be decorated with preprinted
or customized photoprint designs. Children are
naturally fascinated by magnets and Geomag has
been a huge success. Following on, Vincentelli and
Geomag have brought out Baby Magic Attractions,
suitable from 9 months. These larger blocks in semi-
spheres, cubes and discs are easy for toddlers to
handle. They come with rubber animal add-ons and
all can be used in the bath. The colourants are from
food-grade dye; and the shapes are made from non-
toxic Makrolon® and polyurethane.

Lego

Lego, Denmark
www.lego.com

One of the most enduring and
evolving toys, Lego has grown
beyond a brick building toy to
sophisticated construction
applications and advanced
motorized creations. From early
Duplo pieces to the configurations
of themed sets, Bionicles and
Exoforce, and the complex Technic
and robotic Mindstorms, Lego
presents a world of building and
creation that allows children to
follow pattern or embark on their
own designs. Mostly it is loved for
presenting possibilities for more
and different configurations, and
seemingly limitless invention with
the help of cleverly integrated
bright plastic pieces.

Zolo-a-Go-Go

Sandra Higashi, Byron Glaser
Zolo, USA
www.zolo.com

Sandra Higashi and Byron Glaser
first came out with their alternative
building block/character creations
in 1987. The original kits were
distributed by the Museum of
Modern Art, New York, but newer
versions of the Zolo and related
sets are now stocked by various
museum shops and design stores.

BRIO Smart Track & Rechargeable Engines

Isak Åskerlund
BRIO, Sweden
www.brio.net

As well as developing a line of prams and furnishings (see p. 52) BRIO have continued to build on and modernize their classic wooden train sets. The Network system (not shown), devised by Isak Åskerland, is BRIO's first new product launch in over twenty years and adds 'a whole new dimension…a new generation of tracks, toys and wooden characters on a mission from inside your computer'. They have also brought out My First sets and rechargeable engines. Smart Track pieces are embedded with lights and sounds that are activated as a child fits certain pieces together. Even in the face of technology, the wooden railway first produced in 1958 looks ready for play well into the future.

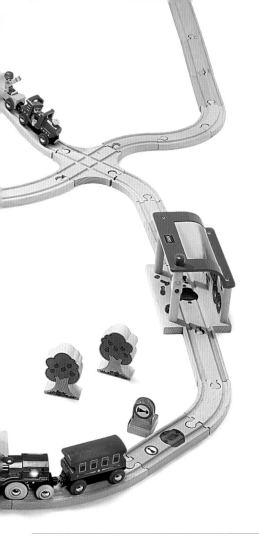

Automoblox Cars

Patrick Calello
Automoblox, USA
www.automoblox.com

This is another one of those toys that will have parents fighting to 'help' the children with. The Automoblox was the brainchild of former industrial designer Patrick Calello, who put his design on the market in 2004 to almost immediate popular appeal. Made from solid wood sourced in Germany, the Automoblox are sets of natural wood blocks with bright plastic connectors and rubber wheels for making (and remaking) toy cars. Passengers fit into different geometric-shaped 'seats' and the parts snap together with an easy click. Combining the enduring appeal of wood and the creative possibilities of interchangeable parts, the Automoblox also feature individual serial numbers, just like real cars, which means they are already being hoarded as collectables.

Streamliner, Xtreamliner, Jetliner

Ulf Hanses, Jangir Maddadi, Sebastian Knorr
Playsam, Sweden
www.playsam.com

'Adults and children write love letters to Playsam,' says CEO Carl Zedig, and it is not difficult to believe him. While there is a plethora of back-to-basics wooden toys on the market, they do not all have nearly the appeal of this touchable little wonder. The high-gloss finish is what first gets your attention, while the shape and size invites little and big hands to pick it up, hold it, rub, polish and play. Wheel mechanisms are pleasantly smooth and the solid wood has a satisfying weight. The Streamliner cars are available with or without little wooden peg passengers. Watch for new, bus, aeroplane and van designs.

Cars, Building Set

Vilac, France

www.vilac.com

Some of the best-loved products created by the
'artisans of Moirans-en-Montagne' for French
toymakers Vilac (see p. 137) are their brightly
coloured, perfectly finished car and transport toys.
Cars for younger children are oversized and honed
to a grippable narrow, but chunky, shape with robust
rubber wheels that can take a good grinding across
the floor. In some, familiar Vilac characters, such as
Rosy the cow, appear to help along with imaginary
play. For slightly older children the vehicles are
smaller and there are the requisite building, fire,
hospital and service station all made from
sustainable wood in the Vilac factory in France.

LikeABike

Rolf Mertens
Kokua, Germany
www.likeabike.com

When he looked at the way we teach children to ride bicycles, using pedals and stabilizers, designer Rolf Mertens discovered that these 'tools' actually prevent children from learning to ride. Many children who are started on bikes with stabilizers end up with bent stabilizers rather than any sense of balance or momentum. Looking back to 1817 when Baron von Drais invented a 'walking machine' that was basically a two-wheeled cycle without pedals, which he moved forward by pushing against the ground, Mertens was inspired. Mertens feels strongly that children learn to balance and move forward much more quickly when they do not have to bother with pedals, and judging by the recent explosion in similar bikes, many people agree. The Mertens family business, Kokua, pioneered the design of pedal-less bicycles and built them from extremely hard-wearing birch and beech ply, which also lends them an irresistible appeal of fine woodcraft and simple, elegant design. The steering has dampers to prevent jackknife spills and seats are all adjustable so that children can start as young as 18 months. A range of models includes the 'race' for indoor spaces, the 'forest' with knobbly off-road tyres and the 'jumper' which has an alloy frame and adjustable rear suspension.

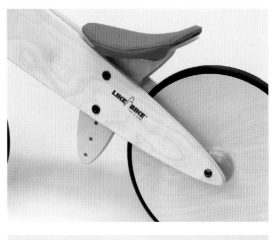

Didicar

Mr Bao
Didicar, China
www.didicar.co.uk

There is a long story about the Didicar that involves a farm in China, an escaped runt piglet, called Didi, and 'the inventor's' discovery that jumping up and down on an old wooden cart made it move forwards. The Didicar originates in China and its forward motion is caused by moving the steering wheel from side to side while applying pressure. It is great for smooth (indoor) surfaces and great fun trying to get up to the maximum 6 mph speed. No one is sure if that is quite fast enough to catch an escaped pig, but the Didicar has won an award for excellence in toy design, 2006.

Black Beauties: Happy Horse, Share Chair, Crash Car

Ineke Hans
Ineke Hans, Netherlands
www.inekehans.com

Black, recycled plastic might not be everyone's first choice for children's products, but Dutch designer Ineke Hans had worked with enough materials to glean its advantages. Being 'wind, water, salt, acid and UV resistant, the material allows products to go outdoors and into wet environments,' says the designer. She also found that 'children not only react to colours,

but very often they respond to shapes, opportunities and ways of playing with things.' In addition to the Happy Horse, Share Chair and Crash Car, Hans has created a highchair (Supperman), desk and chair, skipping rope and other objects for children from the same recycled plastic.

Zolo Ride-on Toys

Sandra Higashi, Byron Glaser
Zolo, USA
www.zolo.com

This enlarged wooden, rideable version of the Zolo-a-Go-Go (see p. 177) was only ever produced in small quantity as the detailing proved too expensive to create for larger distribution. But Sandra Higashi and Byron Glaser's penchant for quirky, inspiring combinations of colour, shape and pattern are all here, and their experimentation continues to inspire more variations in their Zolo play sets.

Olga Rocker, Max Ride On, Lorette Trailer

Wolfgang Sirch, Christoph Bitzer
Sirch, Germany
www.helemill.com

The SIBI range of wooden toys, ride-ons, rockers and push toys are all
made in Bavaria by a woodworking company that has been making
traditional coaches and sledges since the late 19th century. The high
level of craftsmanship, together with a taste for streamlined modern
design, make their products collectors items even for people without any
children to use them. Constructed of laminated birch, ash ply and solid
ash, these sculptural playthings are incredibly sturdy. The wholesome
wood construction and the rounded shapes and colourful details that
make them appealing to the most design-conscious parent are the result
of the successful partnership of Wolfgang Sirch (of the Sirch woodworking
family) and sculptor Christoph Bitzer. Watch for their convertible cot
and highchair launched in 2007.

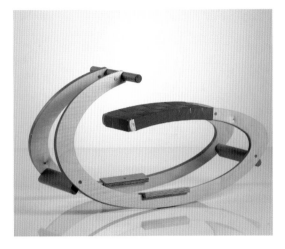

Scuttle Bug

Razor, USA
www.razor.com

Made by the same people who brought out the wildly popular adjustable, folding metal scooter with smooth-riding polyurethane wheels in 2000, the Scuttle Bug is a wonder for little riders from 19 months and up to 20 kg (44 lb). The wheels and steering column all fold and flatten into the body with easy pull-spring mechanisms, making this the ideal trike for travelling with.

Rothan

Isla Rowntree
Islabikes, UK
www.islabikes.co.uk

The smallest of Isla Rowntree's range (see p. 35) for children over 2 years is a beautifully sleek pedal-less bike with pneumatic tyres and low slung 'scoop' saddle. The lightweight aluminium frame is easier for children to manage. Adjustable seat and handlebars, aluminium rims with ball-bearing hubs.

Mini Micro Scooter, G-Bike

Micro Mobility, Switzerland
www.micro-mobility.com

The Swiss designers at Micro Mobility who came out with the Micro
Scooter in 2000 turned their attention to 3–6 year olds in developing
the Mini Micro in 2003. The design is revolutionary in that it is
balanced on three wheels rather than two, which is trickier, or four,
which can be cumbersome, to navigate. The lightweight plastic board
means fewer bruised shins and ankles and easier carrying for children.
The G-Bike, like a scooter with a seat, is for toddlers and helps them to
learn a sense of balance and motion before integrating pedalling.

Greg Lynn
Architect

Founder of the architecture-design practice FORM in Los Angeles, Greg Lynn has defined how architects use computers as a design medium. He was listed among <u>Time</u> magazine's '100 Innovators for the Next Century' and is the author of six books that combine contemporary and popular culture with the rigours of architectural theory and history. He is a Studio Professor at the University of California, Los Angeles, and Davenport Professor at Yale University.

'I like to provoke, stimulate and titillate play by designing things that are a little unprecedented...'

Above middle / Above. Blobwall by Greg Lynn.
Above right. 5900 Wilshire Blvd. Restaurant & Trellis Pavilion, Los Angeles, California.

To what extent do you believe a child's imagination can be stimulated by experimental spatial constructs, whether at the product scale or in an architectural space?
I find my kids like to copy things and they like unfinished things. So giving kids the ability to explore, construct and assemble furniture and environmental scale elements is a plus. Making sure that I am not giving them rote things to copy is also a concern as kids have active imaginations, but they are also childish and they like resolved familiar things. In fact it is very easy to close down future designers by giving

them solutions. Kids will believe almost anything and so pandering to them with simple design solutions is both a danger and the norm.

If design is supposed to be largely functional, what is the function of play in design?
I don't think design is supposed to be largely functional, although all design has to be functional. You can't design a good product by starting and ending with function. There has to be something in between. Play in design can take many forms. I am not very whimsical and I am also not very metaphorical, so these avenues for playfulness are not really where I go. For me play is about putting something into a context and into a use that is not obviously apparent. I like to provoke, stimulate and titillate play by designing things that are a little unprecedented or unfamiliar, but that grow on you both literally and figuratively. I also like the sensuous edge of things in gradient colour, intricate texture and voluptuous form; qualities that invite people to engage with objects in a tactile way.

'Play in design can take many forms.'

What product or existing piece of design would you most like to redesign for children?
Houses, parks, schools and amusement parks.

Great architecture produces 'childlike wonder' – what can architects and designers learn from the way kids see the world?
I think we should be more focused on the values we teach to kids, and wonder is something I think can be learned and fostered. I wouldn't say designers should act like kids. I think we should consider many of these qualities of innovation, experimentation and making something never seen before as mature cultural values and not childish. I know that where my kids go to school they focus on creative critical problem solving and communicating, but they do it in a deadly serious way. The greatest thing about kids is that they all want to do the best things in the world. If you explain to them about cars polluting, the first place they go is designing a car from the ground up. If you explain a site and use for a building the first thing they do is start from the beginning and think through the question in its totality. They don't know much so this is easy for them, but this sensibility of looking at everything all at once is a quality I really admire in kids.

House

Peter Henkes
Kidsonroof, Netherlands
www.kidsonroof.co

This foldable cardboard playhouse was created by
designer Peter Henkes when, he says, 'I tried to find
a present for my then 4-year-old daughter that I could
be engaged in too', but found 'the world of Barbie-
princesses' unexciting. As a result he decided to
make 'a simple, versatile object with an open identity,
that would quickly and organically interact with all
kinds of situations and play.' The A-frame house of
white cardboard has windows, letterbox and doors
cut out and is left blank for customizing/decoration,
which most kids are apt to do even with 'pre-decorated'
structures. A special limited edition Golden House was
added. KOR donate a portion of their profits to Unicef.

Nido

Javier Mariscal
Magis, Italy
www.magismetoo.com

Javier Mariscal made his name with the design of Kobi, the mascot for the Olympic Games in Barcelona in 1992. Now he has a range of designs for Italian furniture manufacturer Magis, whose children's line, Me Too, launched in 2005. Made of rotational-moulded polyethylene, the Nido is one of those toy-furniture hybrids that are becoming very popular in design-conscious families. It is not a storage unit (though you could use it as such); it is not a tent. It is an enclosed place to sit and play, which children, like cats, seem to revel in. With its bright yellow and green plastic form, and protruding eyes and tail, the Nido, or 'nest', looks like an animal about to swallow something, like children bearing toys, snacks and secrets, no doubt. Its floor has a grass pattern and there is graffiti on the underside of the roof. The Nido is suitable for outdoor use, and measures 83 cm high, 150 cm long and 104 cm wide (32 x 59 x 41 in.).

Modern Playshed

Ryan Grey Smith
Velocity Art and Design, USA
www.velocityartanddesign.com

Architect Ryan Grey Smith became known for his prefabricated Modern Shed, which he now sells along with a newer Dwelling Shed and Garden Shed. He has now taken the much-loved structure and brought it down a size in collaboration with Seattle-based design retailers Velocity to create the Modern Playshed. Measuring 223.5 x 112 cm (88 x 44 in.), the shed has all the prefabricated, easy-to-build components, with elements inspired by mid-century architecture: clerestory windows, gently-sloping roof, and stable, or Dutch, doors. It is made from exterior grade fir plywood, prefinished birch, perspex, and all-weather PVC. Optional extras include: deck, coloured exterior panels, floor tiles, interior chalkboard, whiteboard.

Skull Cave

Christopher Robin Nordström
Our Children's Gorilla, Sweden
www.ourchildrensgorilla.com

Combining his avowed love of pop culture and children's whimsy with craftsmanship, Christopher Robin Nordström's take on the play house is suitably odd and irresistibly appealing. (See also pp. 129, 194, 248.) The inspiration came from 'totems, tiki and "the phantom"', according to the designer. Made of sensaten®, a cellular foam material often used for camper's sleeping mats and as an insulating subsurface on roads, which is both lightweight and weatherproof.

3D Hut, Molecule 3, Lem

Harri Koskinen (3D Hut), M+A+P Designstudio (Molecule 3),
ZPZ Partners (Lem)
Play +, Italy
www.playpiu.com

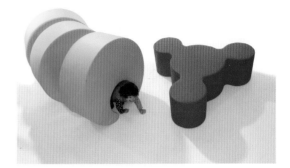

More creative shapes from the collaborative of Play+, Reggio Children and their team of designers (see p. 130). The team under art directors ZPZ Partners make soft furnishings for children to play, learn and imagine. 3D Hut consists of three L-shaped elements with holes which can be combined to form a cubicle, a house or just an open play space. Molecule 3 is soft transformable seating and tunnel shapes that can also be reconfigured. Lem is a shelter with 'eyes' for seeing out or peeping in.

A-Frame

Christopher Robin Nordström
Our Children's Gorilla, Sweden
www.ourchildrensgorilla.com

Inspired by the designs of American architect Andrew
Geller's plans for the A-frame house in the 1950s, this
alternative take on the dolls' house adds modernity
and slightly retro style at the same time. The circular
windows and loft space would give Barbie something
to smile about. The A-frame dolls' house is made of
eco-friendly valchromat® fibreboard. (See also pp.
129, 192, 248.)

SIBI Villa Dolls' House

Wolfgang Sirch, Christoph Bitzer
Sirch, Germany
www.helemill.com

For parents who are true modernists at heart, this
is a mid-century-inspired take on the dolls' house. The
Bauhaus-style toy house was conceived by the pair
behind the range of SIBI toys (see p. 185) and
demonstrates their love of matching traditional woodworking skill with fine contemporary design. The
open-plan Villa features large window walls, garden,
pool and poolhouse and is complete with furniture.

Mobile Home

Peter Henkes
Kidsonroof, Netherlands
www.kidsonroof.com

When designer Peter Henkes created the cardboard House (see p. 190) he formed a company with friend Romy Boesveldt. With four children between them, it is easy to see where their motivation for design derives from. The Mobile Home takes the House concept to another, smaller, level, the doll family home, but improves that object infinitely by making it portable, so dolls can travel to a friend's house for tea, to the park or on holiday.

Thing 3, Lili kitchen

Nico Schweizer
Momoll, Switzerland
www.momoll.com

Nico Schweizer, professor of typography and design and former art director for I.D. magazine, says the ideas for his Thing 3 play tower and Lili kitchen came out of a need to move between two residences while his daughter was young and wanted her favourite toys with her. His aim was to create a flatpack, or collapsible dolls' house and kitchen. However, the end results are as lovely as they are portable. Like all Momoll products, they are made by hand of birch plywood. A set of minimal wood furnishings is available for the Thing 3, along with orange perspex 'windows'. The Lili kitchen comes with optional coloured panels and curtains.

Pookis

Marie Joxe-Collins
Pooki, France
www.pookiandco.com

The trend for weird dolls could
be said to have drawn much of its
inspiration from Marie Joxe-Collins,
a Franco-Colombian illustrator and
brand creator based in France.
Her first dolls were hand-stitched
in 2001 and she is now selling an
extended range of Pookis in three
sizes, along with her handbags,
internationally, largely through
museum and design stores.
Her own influences, she claims,
lie somewhere between the
animated film Yellow Submarine
and Hieronymus Bosch. There
are ten characters, all made from
machine-washable fleece in
Joxe-Collins' own distinctive colours.

Mona Doll

Paco Rabanne
Habitat, UK
www.habitat.net

The fashion designer Paco
Rabanne's contribution to the
Habitat VIP for Kids range
was to make a doll that was as
un-branded as you can get. Apart
from its coloured hair the doll
is a blank slate in the world of
over-made up, hyper-real baby
and fashion dolls. She is also a
nice sturdy shape that is soft
and satisfying to hug. Mona
comes with a set of machine-
washable colouring pens to
decorate her. After washing, she
is ready for another wardrobe
of clothes.

Thilde Doll

Pia Eriksson
Pia Eriksson Textilverkstad, Sweden
www.textilverkstaden.se

The idea behind the Thilde pillow
and rag blanket (see p. 155) also
produced a cushiony fabric doll
with her own assortment of
coloured labels. The Thilde doll
is more like a soft toy, but with
extended arms and legs for easy
dressing up and soft body for
cuddling and holding.

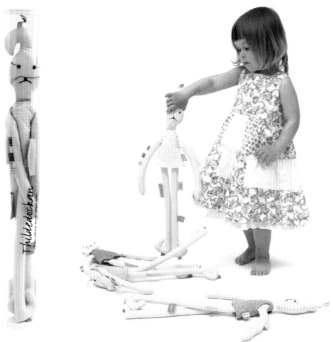

Roomies

Christine Schwarzer,
Anne Birgitte Balle
RoomMate, Denmark
www.roommate.dk

The eponymous dolls created by
the Danish creators of RoomMate
recall the soft simplicity of rag
dolls with a contemporary trend
for slightly offbeat characters.
Ranging from such personalities
as the piratical Fearless Fred and
the accident-prone Pity Paul to
the lawful and unlawful, Chubby
Bobby and Jumping Jack
respectively, Roomies make
comfortably quirky companions.

Bubbles

Pustefix, Germany
www.pustefix.de

In the stark days of postwar Germany a chemist, Dr Rolf Hein,
experimented with washing powder, which he exchanged for food on
the farmlands around Tübingen, and discovered a liquid perfect for
making bubbles. He wanted to create something that would help children
forget the horrors of the war and he produced a complete bubble toy
including liquid, container and blowing tool. Using his children's yellow
teddy bear as his trademark, Hein established the Pustefix bubble toys.

The original Pustefix containers were a small aluminium tube with a
cork stopper with a bubble wand made from metal attached to the cork.
But the metal decomposed after long exposure to soap, and the cork
stopper leaked, so the units did not travel well nor did they have a long
shelf life. It was not until the '60s and the advent of plastics that Dr
Hein's idea really took off and the containers of bubbles could be
exported around the world. Today, the Pustefix company is run by
the third generation of the Hein family and they manufacture bubbles
in sizes from small, disposable sachets, which are great for the park
and outings, to giant bubble exhibitions.

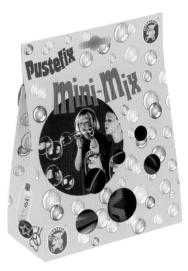

Scrunch Bucket

Funkit World Ltd, UK
www.scrunch-bucket.com

For anyone who has ever been on seaside holiday with
small children the Scrunch Bucket will seem like the
idea that has been waiting to happen. These colourful,
collapsible, foldable containers can be used to mould
sandcastles and fortresses and then cleaned up and
folded away in a car boot or suitcase without breaking.
The 1.5-litre (⅓ gallon) buckets come in six colours.

Flipnfriends

Amanda Levete, Jan Kaplicky, Future Systems
Habitat, UK
www.habitat.net

Contemporary furniture retailers Habitat launched their VIP for Kids range in 2007 with contributions from a range of designers and celebrities. Flipnfriends, a set of interlocking thick clear-coloured acrylic shapes, came about as a way to use up waste material from the Flip tables originally designed by avant-garde British architects Future Systems for the VIP for Kids line (see p. 106). As open-ended puzzles or a bright light mosaic, they make a creative addition to play.

Pixel Blocks

Jay Simmons
Pixel Blocks, USA
www.pixelblocks.com

As a young boy without 'the facility to draw, paint, or sculpt', Jay Simmons felt himself quickly labelled as 'not artistic'. But his problem was dyslexia not a lack of creativity, so he set about finding a way to help others use their creative impulses. Looking at the pixel patterns in a photorealistic tapestry gave him the idea that pictures could be made using numerous blocks of light, which he developed into the tiny attachable pegs that are Pixel Blocks. Like a cross between Lego and Light Brite of old, Pixel Blocks are coloured translucent pieces with ridges and crevices that allow them to be joined side by side, at angles to and on top of each other. They can be used to build structures or just create mosaic-like patterns or pictures that are infused with natural light.

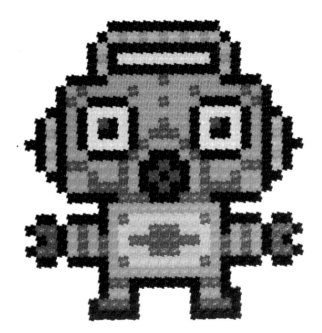

Travel

Changing Bags, Children's Bags, Luggage, Carriers, Backpacks, Travel Cots

Travelling with children is not only about departure lounges and security checks, though these are fraught enough. It is also about trips to granny's house or the grocery store, and with small babies this entails carrying bottles, nappies, wipes, creams, blanket, teddy, an emergency change of clothes and whatever other accessory might make your errand or visit go a bit more smoothly. Along with innovations in buggies, pushchairs/strollers, has come the realization that the old shoulder-slung nappy, or diaper, bag needed improving on. A functional bag for carrying necessities is a must, and the new changing bags are much more versatile. Made of advanced, and in some cases recycled, materials, the latest bags have sturdy, accessible compartments for a range of items and a vigorous sense of style.

Bags for kids have had a makeover in recent years as well, with luggage that is fun, useful and hard-wearing. More manageable, too, are new designs in front-worn and backpack baby carriers. Parents in Western countries have rediscovered the benefits of carrying tiny babies closely wrapped to the body and several makers produce carriers that are easier and more comfortable to use. This is also true of backpack carriers and hip carriers designed for toddlers. Ultimately, the less stressful travel is for babies the more enjoyable it is for parents, which is why travel beds are also important, and here too are new designs for nomadic parents and their offspring.

Expo, Dash & Duo Changing Bags

SKIP*HOP, USA
www.skiphop.com

Husband-and-wife team Ellen and Michael Diamant began their range after becoming new parents and realizing that even in the creative hub of New York city, they were 'surprised by how few products resonated with the urban lifestyle they were used to'. Prized among their creations are the sturdy changing bags in bold, modern colours that offer an array of generous, accessible pockets and compartments, and immensely versatile straps. The wide, robust straps feature Velcro fastenings that allow the bags to be mounted on any pushchair, or stroller, including side-mountings for buggies that tip easily when weight is added to the rear. The strap system also ensures that the bag does not slide down the handle or dangle in front of you. Straps can be adjusted to create a comfortable shoulder strap for messenger-bag carrying when not on the buggy. The Duo has a side mesh pocket for bottles. The Dash has a stylish, foldover closure, and the Expo expands by unzipping the bottom of the bag to extend the main compartment by 50 per cent. The bags come in a variety of colours and patterns.

MotherShip Bag,
Sling Tote,
DJ Bag,
Mobi Stroller Bag

Fleurville, USA
www.fleurville.com

Steve and Catherine Granville set up their company Fleurville to cater to a group of parents who have grown up with a knowledge and sophistication with regard to fashion, branding and child development that the couple felt most makers of children's products were not addressing. Combining their background in design with an understanding of those parents and concerns for the environment, they have produced a line of changing bags, carriers and packs with new materials that are very effective and also environmentally sensitive. Their Sling Tote, MotherShip Bag and mini Escape Pod are covered in brightly coloured textiles and then sealed in PVC-free plastic that keeps the rain out and is totally wipe-clean. Their newer bags are covered in unique Green-LAM®, a 'very environmentally friendly polyurethane laminate', which is moisture- and UV-resistant and free of PVC. The Mobi Stroller or pushchair Bag is a cool-looking utilitarian satchel in Fleurville's proprietary fabric, Re-Run, made from recycled plastic bottles. It has a trendy box shape and wide shoulder strap and is designed to carry nappies or diapers, bottles, wipes and assorted baby paraphernalia; the DJ Bag is similar, with a single strap backpack designed for dads. Most of the bags come with 'O-rings' that allow them to be securely attached to pushchair, or stroller handles, as well as changing cloths, zippered compartments, internal carabiner/key clips and adjustable shoulder straps.

Dad Field Bag

Jack Spade, USA
www.jackspade.com

For new-age dads or just anyone who wants to carry baby gear in a slightly more stylish, masculine vessel, the bagmakers at Jack Spade have turned their talents to a high-quality changing bag for men. Made from water-resistant, 1100 denier-weave nylon canvas, the Field Bag has an exterior zipper pocket for audio player, audio port for headphones, phone pocket, back pocket, interior compartments with soccer-pitch changing pad and an adjustable shoulder strap.

Nursery Bag

Mutsy B.V., Netherlands
www.mutsy.com

After Freek Driessen took over the Dutch company Mutsaerts, which became Mutsy in 1994, from his father, Cees, the look and scope of the brand began to change. Mutsy now offer a comprehensive range of travel systems (see pp. 24–5) as well as highchairs and baby seats (pp. 61, 72). No travel system is complete without a well-designed changing bag and Mutsy have delivered that too in a variety of styles, all with a modern edge and bold contemporary colours.

Carry-all, Hobo

OiOi, Australia
www.oioi.com.au

This increasingly popular
Australian brand was born
when founder Lisa Bennetts,
who formerly worked in product
development and marketing for
handbags, had a child of her
own. Eschewing the idea that a
changing bag has to be somehow
decorated like a nursery, she soon
created her first messenger bag.
OiOi continue to make baby bags
using the patterns and colours of
new season handbags and offer a
range from large totes to small
backpacks, all fashionably formed.

Zoo Bags

Christine Schwarzer,
Anne Birgitte Balle
RoomMate, Denmark
www.roommate.dk

Christine Schwarzer and Anne
Birgitte Balle's designs for children's
bags are bright, fun and durable.
Made of cotton with felt animal
appliqué design they demonstrate
the design duo's aim to create
products that appeal to children
and inject a bit of fun into the adult
world (see also p. 197). Backpack,
shoulder and cosmetic bags come
in four colourways and prints. They
also produce matching t-shirts.

Marsupial, Bandicoot, Zoom Kit, Go Tote

Johanna Leestma LaFleur
Loom, Inc, USA
www.loomlife.com

Loom was founded in the spring of 2003 by Johanna Leestma LaFleur. LaFleur has played with fabric, print, and colour since her early childhood but she says it was her experiences living in Senegal, Sweden, Thailand and Hong Kong that have further fed her interest in textile and pattern. Loom changing bags and totes are all made from high-quality, contrasting-coloured nylon with rugged construction, padded handles and reinforced seams. They have functional pockets for storing bottles, nappies and other items, and feature clever combinations, such as the Bandicoot's smaller, removable bag. The Marsupial adheres to the 'one hand/no eyes' concept meaning that everything is easily accessible and the bag is sturdy enough to handle vigorous rummaging.

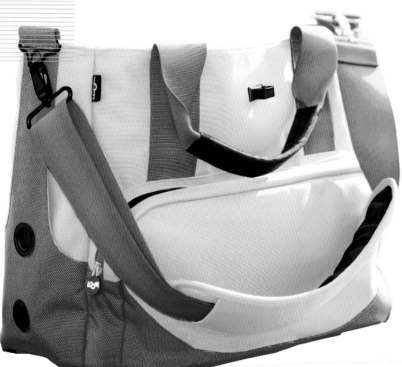

Trunki

Rob Law
Magmatic Ltd, UK
www.trunki.co.uk

Trunki first came to public awareness in the UK when designer Rob Law appeared on the television programme Dragon's Den in which entrepreneurs present ideas to a panel of investors and try to convince them to take an interest in their products. Much to their later chagrin, the 'Dragons' refused to take part in Law's budding company, though after the programme was recorded one investor did ask to purchase two Trunkis for his children. Today Law can hold his head up high as his design for the world's first children's ride-on suitcase is recognized in the UK, USA and Europe for its design and has garnered a number of awards. The Trixie and Terrance (pink and blue versions) have been followed by the Towgo or Posh Trunki that features inside straps and pockets.

Timber Kids

Samsonite, UK
www.samsonite.com

Produced under licence by Samsonite, the Timberland range of luggage for children, Timber Kids, includes backpacks, wheeled packs, upright trolley cases, duffels, lumbar packs and accessories in a range of interesting colours (orange persimmon, yellow, pink rubia, rhododendron [red], navy and emerald green). The range features heavy Timberland branding, but also expresses the ruggedly stylish concept people have come to expect from Timberland. The bags are constructed of hard-wearing canvas with covered zips, polyurethane wheels, chunky telescoping handles and numerous pockets and pouches for all manner of travel necessities.

Ultrabike, Junior, Waldfuchs

Deuter, Germany
www.deuter.com

When it was founded in 1898 the Deuter company made mail sacks for the Bavarian Royal Mail. The company went on to specialize in objects made of sail cloth, such as tents and backpacks for the military. Throughout the 20th century Deuter became known for producing hard-wearing outdoor equipment for expeditions and, later, sporting events. Today, working with the most advanced fabrics they produce some of the world's best-known outdoor gear, including products for children (see also p. 219). The Ultrabike is a brightly coloured, shaped backpack with integrated Blink light, and front and rear reflectors. The Junior is designed 'for kindergarten, swimming and mountain adventures' with reflectors, soft-padded back and shoulders and child-friendly buckles. The Waldfuchs is designed to hold all the kit little foresters need, including a foam seat mat.

Little Lifestyles

Little Lifestyles, UK
www.little-lifestyles.com

Little Lifestyles present a range of sophisticated designs for bags that are full of features to make carrying baby accessories free of hassle. The Little Linea collection, designed in Italy by Escudama, has textured fabric with two-tone styling and oversized zip pulls, as well as changing mat, bottle holders and detachable straps. The Little Leisures City bags have large external buckled pockets and multiple internal pockets as well as a textured base to keep the bottom of the bag from getting dirty when placed on the ground. Both the Holdall and the Compact styles have coordinated changing mats and the Compact has two elasticated straps to attach to a pushchair, or stroller.

Little Packrats Backpacks

Cathy Berse-Hurley
CBH Studio, USA
www.cbhstudio.com

Drawing on her art education and first-hand knowledge of what appeals to children, designer Cathy Berse-Hurley makes packs with bold graphic images of animals in vivid contrasting colours that feature well-crafted details such as coordinating patterns on the reverse side of the pack and 3D protruding ears, tails, or a lion's mane. The backpacks are made in extremely durable, colourful, washable vinyl.

Líllébaby EuroTote

Líllébaby, USA
www.lillebaby.com

Following recent research suggesting that newborns should be allowed to lie flat rather than awkwardly propped in old-style car seats, the Líllébaby EuroTote is meant to provide a cushioned portable support that lets babies lie in the preferred flat position while being carried. Arguments for the prone position cite spinal development, better circulation and better environment for sleep during travel. The EuroTote, modelled on European-style carriers, is made of a quilted microfibre outer layer and a 100 per cent cotton lining with a carrying board for spinal support. Yet it is multifunctional: through zips and clasps it can be converted from a carrier to a bunting bag, pushchair or stroller liner, play blanket and travel bedding that fits directly into car seats. These functions also mean that the carrier can continue to be used long after the child has outgrown the carrier stage.

Cocoon

phil&teds, New Zealand
www.philandteds.com

Used on its own as a baby carrier
or clipped into the phil&teds
Sport buggy, the Cocoon is a snug
padded sleep sack for babies. The
base is padded and the headrest
has adjustable toggles to keep out
draughts. Long loop handles for
carrying, or swaying, and full-
length zips make it easy to get
baby settled in. Cocoon is covered
in washable waterproof fabric and
comes in seven colours. It is
suitable for babies from newborn
up to 6 months.

Hipseat

Hippychick, UK
www.hippychick.com

Easily classed under the rubric of products that just
make sense, the Hippychick Hipseat solves the age-old
problem of heavy, tired toddlers and their equally
tired parents when a buggy or pushchair is just not
an option. The Hipseat is a padded foam shelf for the
baby to sit on that is held around the waist using a
wide, back-supporting belt. The makers say it was
'specifically designed to address one of the root
causes of adult back pain' by allowing the adult's back
to remain straight as they hold the child on the hip,
rather than slanting to one side. Encased in durable
Cordura fabric with secure inner pockets, the belts
are machine-washable. The Hipseat has proved
particularly popular in England where the National
Trust (caretakers of historic houses) loan them out
to visiting parents.

Polygloo

Matali Crasset
Pinpon, France
www.club-pinpon.com

French product designer Matali Crasset (see pp. 104-5, 123) has come up with another striking innovation for children, a baby carrier that is both practical and bold. The fabric can be changed to suit summer or winter weather. For winter the cover is a type of neoprene with a 3D mesh inside. For summer there is a nylon parachute material with 3D mesh also inside. The Polygloo features a bright range of colours, an ample protective hood and wide crisscrossing straps for comfort.

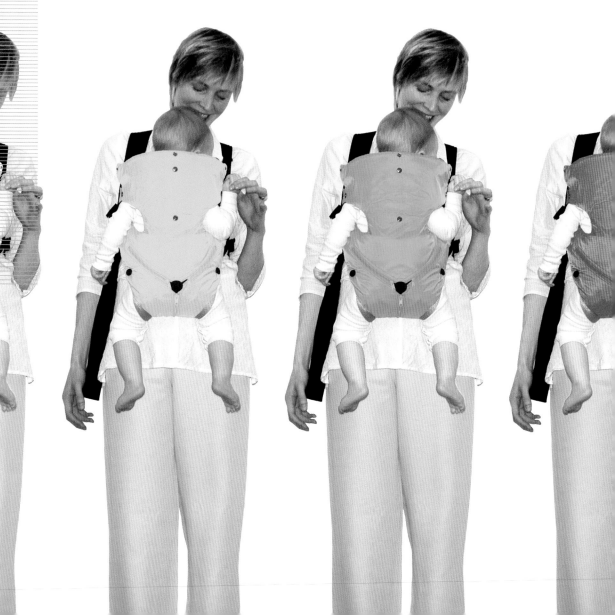

Zucco

Aprica, Italy
www.aprica-italia.it

Convertible carriers are the new must-have item for
mums and dads. For those who are not skilled
at wrapping themselves and their infant in a long
piece of cloth, as another trend has it, an easy-to-use,
comfortable, adaptable baby carrier is a nursery
necessity. Italian manufacturers Aprica have introduced
a range of carriers from the minimal Quick, which
is like a front mounted handbag, to the new Zucco,
which can be worn with either baby facing forward
or inward, as a backpack carrier or cradling the baby
across your front. It is truly adaptable, and suitable
for children from birth to 3 years (15 kg/33 lb).

Quinny Curbb

Quinny/Dorel, Netherlands
www.quinny.com

One item that designers of children's products seem
intent to improve on is the baby/toddler carrier.
Quinny's answer is the Curbb carrier, which is partly
a hip seat and partly a strapped carrier. The Curbb is
designed to fit on the hip while supported by shoulder
straps across the front and back.

Samsonite Rival Baby Carrier

Doris Fricke-Reimann, Fiona Woodhead
Weybury Hildreth/Samsonite, UK
www.baby-travel.com

To make the Rival quicker to fasten and easier to use than many baby carriers, the designers minimized the number of straps and buckles. It opens on one side only and the side panels are firm but elasticated, to stretch as the baby grows. Made of padded ripstop nylon the Rival also features a removable pod to support smaller babies, zipped front storage pocket and detachable dribble bib. The lining is 100 per cent cotton jersey.

Original, Active & Air Carrier

Björn Jakobson, Lillemor Jakobson
BabyBjörn, Sweden
www.babybjorn.com

When Björn Jakobson designed his first baby carrier in the early 1970s, there was a lot of interest in carrying babies close to the body, he explains, but only one carrier available, which was a Japanese product. Jakobson went on to create generations of carriers: in 1987 it was a new carrier that fastened in the front instead of the back; in 1996 it was the use of black fabric. With thirty years of experience BabyBjörn continue to innovate, offering the Original, front-fastening design, which was developed in consultation with parents and medical experts, along with the Active Carrier, for heavier babies, and the lighter Air Carrier.

Escape Backpack

phil&teds, New Zealand
www.philandteds.com

Ever since the idea was first put forward to make a child's carrier that was useful for hiking, hill-walking or just going places a pushchair, stroller or buggy cannot go, there have been variations and improvements. The Escape has as many features as you could possibly get on a child carrier and still keep it portable: adjustable harness, adjustable seat, foot stirrups, adjustable child harness, multiple storage pockets, clip-off child's day pack, rear-vision mirror, sun cover with rollout rain flaps, changing mat with pouch and removable dribble cloth. Amazingly, the whole contraption can be folded flat for storage and only weighs 2 kg (4½ lb). (There is also a less extensive Metro version for shorter journeys.)

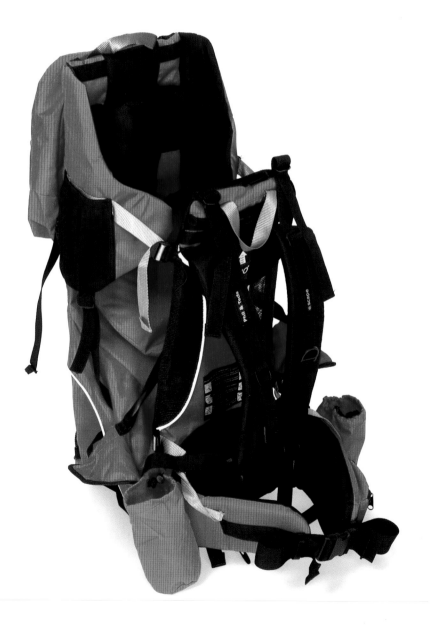

Kids Carrier

Nomad, Netherlands
www.nomad.nl

Carrying a child on your back can be a tricky business whether you are out for a day's hike or a day's shopping. The Nomad carrier is a serious piece of kit. With padded hip rests, straps and back panels, it has multiple 'back-length' adjustments for different wearers. For the child's comfort, the padded high-backed 'cockpit' can also be adjusted to various sizes, up to 15 kg (33 lb). An optional sunroof/rain cover and head rest can be attached. There is an easy-access rear pouch and an ample underseat storage pocket with carrier bag. The sturdy folding bar stand means the pack can be set down securely for rest stops.

Together Carrier

Aprica, Italy
www.aprica-italia.it

Another clever design from Italian makers Aprica is this rear or forwards facing child-carrier and portable child seat in one. Comprised of two pieces that fit together, its top half is removable and has extending arms to fit it snugly to a tabletop for dining out. The bottom portion holds the roomy day pack with two exterior zipper compartments for quick access to essentials such as tissues or snacks. The carrier has padded lumbar support and adjustable straps. It is suitable for children from 9 to 36 months (7–16 kg/ 15 ½–35 lb).

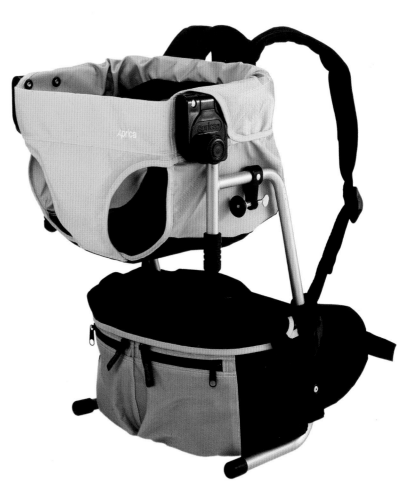

Voyager, Ultralight

LittleLife, UK
www.littlelife.co.uk

From a company set up to manufacture equipment for expeditions and adventure travel, the designers at LittleLife have found a receptive audience for their practical and brightly styled child carriers and tent beds. The Voyager is their most deluxe child carrier, with a removable rear-attached 'daysack' that can be carried separately or clipped to the front of the carrier for easier access. The design of the carrier is 'taken from top-level mountaineering rucksacks and ensures maximum carrying comfort over long periods'. The 'anatomically shaped child seat' comes with a decorative soft face-protection pad for the child to rest against and toy loops. It also includes side mesh pockets for drinks and a large base pocket, as well as top and side handles and mirror for checking on the child behind you. The Ultralight is the company's most compact and lightweight model, but is still sturdy with clips for attaching foot stirrups. It folds almost flat and comes with its own carry bag. Both models are suitable from 6 months to 4 years.

Vamoose

Macpac, New Zealand
www.macpac.co.nz

Among outdoor lovers, Macpac is a well-loved and highly respected maker of packs and carriers. Among their models of child carriers, the Vamoose is a luxury transport kind of product. The base has a 25-litre storage compartment, and a day pack at the back can be zipped off for separate use. The face pad is also removable (and washable), as are the child harness straps. Most importantly the Explorer™ load-carrying system uses various adjustable straps, hip belt, internal frame bar and lumbar cushion to ensure that the wearer has the pack properly fitted to help with balance, keep pressure points from forming and make sure the weight is evenly distributed.

Kid Comfort II, III

Deuter, Germany
www.deuter.com

Deuter have been making outdoor gear for over one hundred years (see p. 208) and their newest products demonstrate the experience and craft of their history. The child carriers have all the advantages of modern advances and a few more. The Kid Comfort II features a Vari-Quick adjustment system that does away with contorted threading and pulling on straps, and anatomically shaped shoulder straps. A side-entry system means children can be settled in or out of the carrier without removing it. The Kid Comfort III delivers more comfort with Vari-Flex hip fins. Both have a higher padded headrest, zipped outer pockets and removable extra soft pillow.

Venus

Croft & Fisher
Bushbaby, UK
www.bush-baby.com

The first carrier designed by women specifically for women, the Venus is one of the latest innovations in the Bushbaby family of carriers and accessories. Its size allows for the difference in a woman's body shape and proportions. It has a loading leg for stability, a shorter back length and a 'Bigeye back-system', which allows for quick and easy adjustment while carrying. In addition, the shoulder straps are contoured to fit curves, the hip belt has mesh cutaways to hug the hips and there is increased head support for baby, as well as a fleece child seat, and a number of enhanced details and accessories.

Koo-di Pop-up Bubble

Doris Fricke-Reimann
Weybury Hildreth/Koo-di, UK
www.koo-di.co.uk

A very compact, light and easy-to-assemble alternative to the larger framed travel cot, the Koo-di Pop-up Bubble is also a bright modern piece of gear. Using a flexible wire structure covered in washable poly-cotton fabric and polyester mesh, the Pop-up grows from 60 x 30 x 18 cm (23 ½ x 12 x 7 in.) in a compact carrycase to a bed of 96 x 82 x 60 cm (37 ½ x 32 x 23 ½ in.). Ideal for occasional use during day trips and visits, the Koo-di is quick to set up and is suitable from birth to about 18 months.

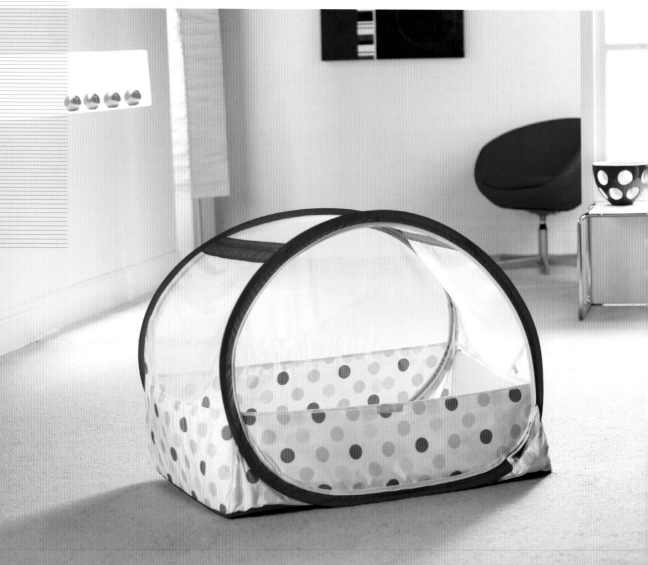

Samsonite Pop-up Travel Cot Deluxe

Doris Fricke-Reimann
Weybury Hildreth/Samsonite, UK
www.baby-travel.com

The small design and manufacturing company Weybury Hildreth creates nursery products for a number of labels. The Samsonite Pop-up Cot was designed by Doris Fricke-Reimann and adheres to Samsonite standards of durability and neutral luggage tones, but its features are more dynamic. The Pop-up Travel Cot Deluxe can pop into shape in seconds, and collapses into a small, circular shape that measures only 28 cm (11 in.) in diameter, and weighs under 1 kg (2¼ lb). The main fabric and mattress are made of 100 per cent cotton with a polyester mesh net. As with the Koo-di (opposite), wire framing with a system of small metal struts make the firm but flexible structure. The assembled cot measures 89 x 56 x 50 cm (35 x 22 x 20 in.) and includes loops for attaching small toys. A coordinated sleeping bag and soft jersey sheets are available.

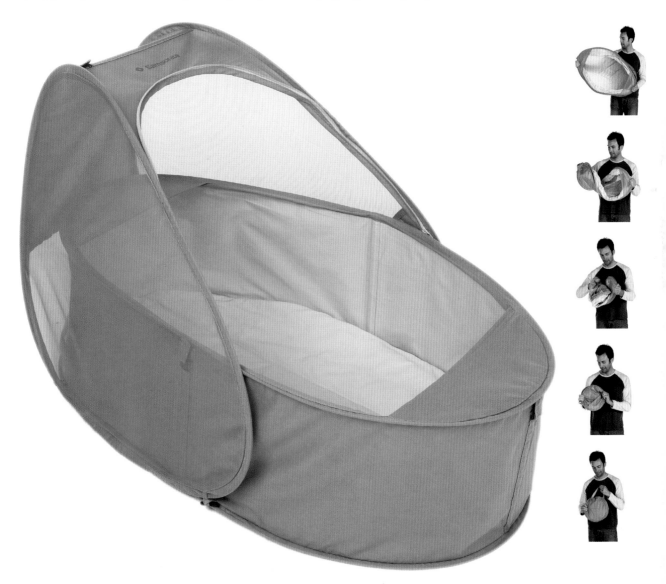

Baby Travel

Delta Diffusion, Belgium
www.deltababy.be

A highly compact, multifunctional and practical
answer to travelling with babies, the Baby Travel
is Delta Diffusion's baby luggage and bed all-in-one.
As a travel bed it features a soft, cosy nest with outer
pockets for essentials. The four large compartments
fasten securely for travel. One of these has an
isothermal cover to maintain food/liquid temperature
and inserts to hold bottles in the upright position when
the bag is carried. Closed up for travel, it becomes a
fairly lightweight shoulder bag suitable for carrying
nappies, wipes, spare clothes and toys.

Nomad Kids Travel Bed

Nomad, Netherlands
www.nomad.nl

The outdoor company Nomad have
extended their range to carriers
and tents for children. This tent
bed is an easy-to-assemble structure
consisting of one whole-piece nylon
and mesh tent with zipped mesh
openings and two expandable rods.
The rods click together to make two
long arcs and are inserted through
crisscrossing seams whose tension
pulls the nylon structure taut.
Straps attached to the pole inserts
at each corner help to adjust the
tension. A separate mattress is also
available. The tent bed can be used
outdoors, but with its compact
lightweight carry bag it makes a
convenient travel bed for overnight
visits just about anywhere.

T2 Travel Cot

phil&teds, New Zealand
www.philandteds.com

Weighing only 2 kg (4 ½ lb) is the compact, easy to set up T2 travel cot, which is an essential item for any parents who want to get away and be able to sleep at night. The T2 also has a UV shade cover and pegs for outdoor use. The angled legs make the lightweight frame very sturdy. For use up to 3 years.

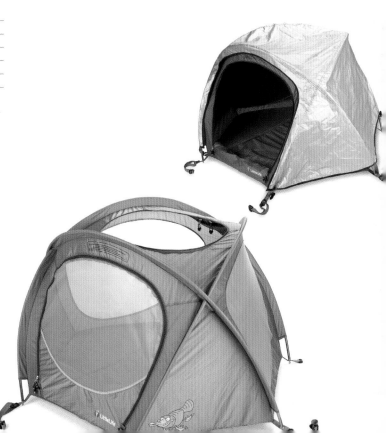

Arc-3 Travel Cot

Little Life,UK
www.littlelife.co.uk

Little Life specialize in carriers and outdoor products for children. The latest addition to their travel bed/tent range is a new shape and three-pole design that allows more flexibility with indoor space, a roomier interior and greater structural strength. Made of lightweight aluminium poles and ripstop nylon fabric the Arc 3 is easy to assemble and very portable. The mesh top and front-opening sunshade are included.

Travel Crib Light

BabyBjörn, Sweden
www.babybjorn.com

BabyBjörn have a solid reputation for quality baby products (see p. 215) and their new Travel Crib Light is possibly the most lightweight and easiest to use travel cot now on the market. Constructed of soft nylon fabric with mesh panels that allow you to see into the cot from around the room, the bed is ready in one movement. As it you unfold the two hinged halves, the sprung leg framework locks firmly into place. The crib weighs 5 kg (11 lb) in its carrying bag, and includes mattress and cover.

Kaboost

Amir Levin
Kaboost, USA
www.kaboost.com

Designer Amir Levin had the idea of making chairs more suitable for young children to sit in rather than giving them child-size versions after a family meal with his young cousins. He noticed that the younger ones wanted to sit in proper chairs like their older siblings and were not happy using booster seats. The Kaboost, which he launched in 2007, is a secure device for raising the level of almost any four-legged chair up by almost 9 x 11.5 cm (3 ½ to 4 ½ in.), similar to most boosters. The spring-loaded arms hold the chair legs in place and non-slip rubberized feet keep the chair stable. The Kaboost is portable and there is no assembly required.

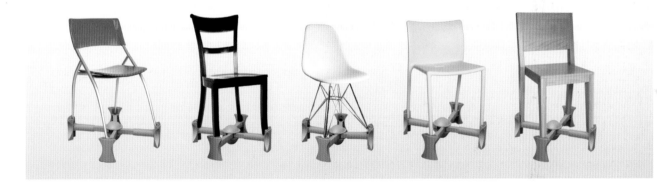

Metoo

phil&teds, New Zealand
www.philandteds.com

An incredibly lightweight, portable and functional travel seat for children from the designers behind one of the most innovative and fun collections of gear for children (see pp. 210, 216, 223), the Metoo weighs less than 1 kg (2 ¼ lb) and fits handily in the parcel compartment of the Sport buggy (p. 29). It is made of washable nylon fabric with an aluminium frame that clamps on to most tabletops. From 6 months to 3 years (18 kg/40 lb).

Night Lights, Fun Lights & Lamps, Equipment

As electronics become more advanced, the devices used for children become safer, more robust and adaptable. Babies' rooms need general lighting as well as a soft light for night-time feeds and changes. Young children often want some light source in their room when they sleep, and it is useful if that can be a low, glowing light. Some people advocate lamps that move or splash scenes across the walls and ceiling, while others feel such things provide too much stimulation. The most innovative products are the new rechargeable lamps that stay cool to the touch and can be safely handled by small children, as they have no wires that can be tangled or damaged. These lamps are now being produced in child-friendly shapes that give them the appearance of gently glowing cuddly toys. Some lighting designers have experimented with shape and colour without specifically designing for children, but have found that these more unusual designs appeal to parents who are looking for ways to introduce some creative atmosphere to their children's rooms.

From lighting to devices that are aimed at safety and security, the designers of electronics for children are racing ahead in every category producing gadgets that are far more advanced than even a few years ago. Humidifiers have taken shape as aesthetic objects, and baby monitors now offer video as well as audio functions. Monitors, now a nursery necessity, are being enhanced with digital technology and now have the look and capability of sophisticated surveillance equipment, in ever smaller packages.

Star Egg Nightlight

Jim Schatz
J Schatz, USA
www.jschatz.com

The brightly coloured, highly polished orb looks like an oversized sweet, but was created as part of Jim Schatz' growing line of egg-inspired product designs. However, children's retailers and parents have seized on it as the perfect nursery illuminator. After ten years 'experimenting with the ovoid shape', Schatz hit on the egg as a night light, with numerous holes poked in the ceramic shell to create a starry scattering across the room at night. Unfortunately, it is hot to the touch if a bulb of greater than 25 watts is used. Available in light aqua, sun yellow, pink, orange peel, olive, red hot, ginger, dark tide pool, silver grey and white.

Candeloo

Vessel, USA
www.vesselstore.com

Developed by innovative Massachusetts-based lighting
company Vessel, the Candeloo provides soft, safe
lighting that is fully accessible to children. The lights
come in a set of two with a charger. After the lamp
is charged it can glow for up to eight hours. The two-
lamp system means one can charge while another
is used. The lamps stay cool to the touch and so
are safe for children to carry around on trips to
the bathroom or to check what is under the bed. In
addition, the patented SafeCharge™ system
eliminates exposed electrical contacts, so there
is no danger of children touching bare elements.

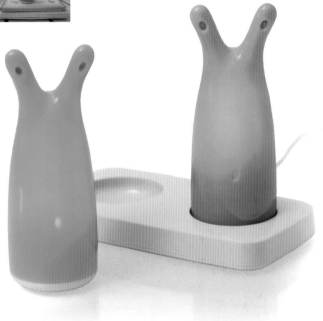

Lumilove

Lumilove
Pabobo, France
www.pabobo.com

Pabobo, a company that started out designing
educational games for children, claim to be the original
creators of the portable night lamp. These five
creatures 'from the planet Zunion' are rechargeable
and last for up to eight hours, changing colour while
they glow. With low-energy LED lights, they are safe
for small children and can even sit in bed with them.

Nightlight with Warm Mist Humidifier, Wireless Video Camera Monitor, Travel Monitor

NScessity, UK
www.nscessity.co.uk

Liz Newton founded NScessity, still a small company, only a few years ago but they have emerged at the forefront of electronics for babies. The Nightlight with Warm Mist Humidifier combines two essential baby room functions in one well-designed unit. The Travel Monitor is a smaller version of the device, which comes in a carrying case and can operate on batteries only, for remote retreats. The Video Camera Monitor has a 6.3 cm (2 ½ in.) screen, 4 channels and infra-red sensor, so you can see baby in the dark and decide whether the noise they are making is worth running for. The camera is fully adjustable, wall mountable and has 150 m range. Additional cameras can be purchased for different rooms. Watch for NScessity's digital video monitor, which will be available in late 2008.

Light Monster,
Light Dragon,
Light Garland

HABA, Germany
www.haba.de

More treats from the vast HABA store of children's
products, the fantastical creature lights, such as the
Light Monster and Light Dragon. These are basic
poseable desklamps that feature a coloured wooden
base and bulb casing, and a bright nylon sack covering
that gives squishy animal shape and overall animation
to the utilitarian object. The Light Dragon can even
'curl up' next to your bed. Light Garland (not shown)
is a string of flowery plastic petals but with HABA
quality fittings and a cone-shaped container to create
a light bouquet.

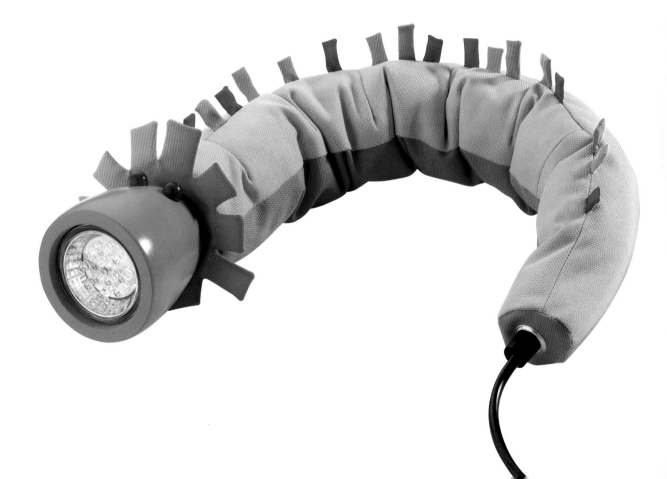

John Maeda
Head, MIT Media Lab

World-renowned designer, visual artist and computer scientist, John Maeda became the 16th president of the prestigious Rhode Island School of Design in 2008. Former Associate Director of Media Arts & Sciences at the Media Lab of the Massachusetts Institute of Technology in Cambridge, Massachusetts, Maeda was a founding voice for 'simplicity' in the digital age.

'Design things as unfinished and broken objects. Let the children themselves make them whole.'

Above. Eye'm hungry, 2005
Right. Nature, 2004

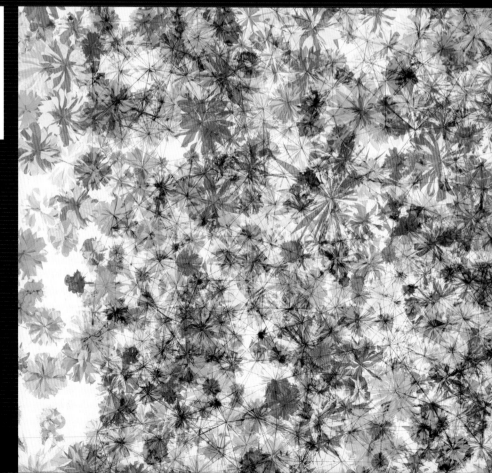

In its simplicity and beautiful utility, design when it is great can produce 'childlike wonder' – what can designers learn from the way kids see the world?

Designers can learn from children how to forget about everything they already know and aspire to recall a world where all that really mattered ... was the next time you would have a snack. And even more importantly, WHAT that snack might be. Children care little about whether their jumper is Prada or the table they sit at is by Eames. They only care about eating, sleeping, and pooping. Is there anything else to life?

For decades – back to Bruno Munari, the Eameses, and beyond – many great designers and architects have created objects, furniture, books and spaces for kids. For some it has even been an integral part of their design process. Is this still true today? If not, what could designers today learn from these practices?

The simple answer is yes. The complex answer is 'who can afford the vast lines of upscale designer goods "for kids"?'. Having grown up with limited means as a child, I can't say that designer goods for children are must-haves to the extent that they are marketed in the world. But they're not bad to have around at all.

In an age of instant digital gratification, what do you think is the most important consideration in designing for kids today?

Recognizing that even the simplest object is the result of a complex chain of creative thoughts and industrial processes; that each object in our surrounds literally connects us with thousands of people – and, in the case of the Web, billions.

Given that a child's perception is much more 'pure' than that of an adult jaded by decades of consumerism, is it possible for a child to differentiate between 'design', 'experience' and 'emotion'?

I have no idea. Ask a child.

Kids are by nature 'interactive', so that 'designing for kids' can often be a redundant act. It is the simplest things – balls, pots and pans, bean bags – that kids return to time and time again. How can we make interactivity that takes kids to another realm of experience?

Design things as unfinished and broken objects. Let the children themselves make them whole.

Do you have a personal favourite toy or object and why does it appeal to you?

My favourite toy is a little branch with a propeller atop its trunk. The branch has ridges on it that when rubbed against, for some odd reason the propeller spins.

TwistTogether Lamp

Steve Feuerborn, David Liatti
Glide, Inc, USA
www.thetwistogetherlamp.com

Made of separate units that can be stuck together in a myriad of combinations of coloured squares and a cartoon figure who parades over and around them all, the TwistTogether Lamp makes making light a creative activity. Designer Steve Feuerborn says the inspiration was 'a pretty basic idea – wouldn't it be great if you could "pluck" light out of the air and rearrange it however you please?' It would; it is.

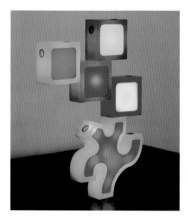

Moonbuzz

Buzz Aldrin
Habitat, UK
www.habitat.net

Glowing moons, planets and stars are a favourite design scheme for the ceilings of many children's bedrooms, so astronaut Buzz Aldrin's idea for Habitat VIP for Kids was always going to be popular. 'It's no big secret that I'm fascinated by the moon. So when I was approached to contribute to the range I knew exactly what I wanted to achieve,' says the moon walker. The Moonbuzz is a pendant lamp made from white resin cast in an accurate 3D replica of the moon's surface. Buzz Aldrin has also authored a children's book, Reaching for the Moon.

TykeLight Buddy

Mobi, USA
www.getmobi.com

Soft, ambient light in another clever portable, rechargeable unit cast in a friendly shape for children, the TykeLight Buddy makes night light not only comforting, but happy. It is handy for a bedside friend or a night-time trip to the bathroom. Made of impact-resistant plastic with built-in rechargeable batteries, it is safe to hold and clean, and the automatic on/off will come on automatically during power cuts when it is sitting in the recharger. It comes in six colours.

Resin Cube Lights

Kari Merkl
Merkled, USA
www.merkled.com
www.velocityartanddesign.com

Kari Merkl is an industrial designer with a background in architecture and fabrication. She started making her resin cube lights in 2004 and though they were never aimed specifically at the children's market, she found that they became popular with parents looking for cool, interesting additions to their children's bedrooms. She still makes each light by hand in her workshop in Portland, Oregon, USA.

Autofade Lamp

Babytec International Products Ltd, UK
www.babytec.co.uk

Helping babies and children adjust to the routine of being put to sleep on their own is a fraught exercise. Light is often a key to comfort, so the creators at Babytec have come up with a soft-light lamp that fades slowly over a period of fifteen minutes from full illumination to darkness, allowing the child to become used to lower light gradually until the light is off or they fall asleep. Made of standard ABS, the Autofade stays cool to the touch, has a touch-sensitive dimmer switch and is 18 cm (7 in.) high, with a 25-watt supply.

Blimp, Big Blimp, Minilamp

Mathmos, UK
www.mathmos.com

Design-led lighting manufacturers Mathmos, the inventors of the Lava Lamp, are another group who have found themselves appealing to children and parents without really meaning to. However, one look at the Blimp, Mini or Ghost lamps and anyone struggling to find something just a little quirky for the kids is immediately smitten. The lamps are part of the Mathmos Softlights series and use LED lights, which keep the surface of the lamps cool to the touch. They change colour through the full spectrum using the latest technology. Lights are turned on and off by gently pressing down on the cover. Each light is made from mouth-blown glass, so they are probably more safely activated by parents or older children.

Grobag Egg

Grobag, UK
www.grobag.com

Concerns about the causes of cot death or SID (sudden infant death syndrome) have engendered a whole new industry of products designed to reduce known or suggested risks. The Grobag Egg, however, is useful without being needlessly intrusive. There are no alarms, bells or whistles involved, simply a softly glowing night light that changes colour according to room temperature. A pleasant yellow colour indicates ideal temperature but will grow to orange and then red if the atmosphere is too warm for the baby. Blue, though a lovely hue, means the room is too cold. A digital readout shows the actual temperature. Even if the room temperature is fairly stable and adequate, the Grobag makes a pleasant and comforting nursery-room night light.

DECT Baby Monitor, LivingColours Lamp

Philips, Netherlands
www.philips.com

Royal Philips Electronics is one of the largest electronics companies in the world so it is only natural that they should be at the forefront of new technology for the nursery as well as the home. The DECT digital monitor provides a secure private connection to the baby's room by automatically changing channels if another device is detected on the same frequency. The remote unit is rechargeable, gives a reading of the room temperature and has a 300 m (984 ft) range. The base unit can play five lullabies and makes a lighted star pattern. The LivingColours lamp is a remote-controlled unit that lets you change the colour and intensity of light for any room but can be particularly useful when trying to light a baby or child's room, when the pale pink, blue or violet hues can be used to softly light a wall, ceiling or corner and dimmed or turned off when baby goes to sleep.

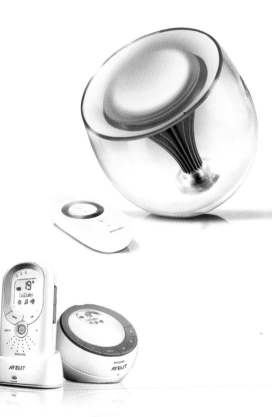

Humidifier Ver.3

Naoto Fukasawa
Plusminuszero, Japan
www.dynamism.com

Designer Naoto Fukaswa was part of the early group
behind IDEO and helped set up IDEO Japan before
joining the advisory board for Muji, for whom he
created the award-winning wall-hung CD player.
Among his graceful, slimmed-down designs for
his company Plusminuszero, the doughnut-shaped
humidifier has drawn fans among many parents
who often use humidifiers to keep babies' rooms
from drying out and causing night-time stuffiness.
Though not a conscious kids' design the playful,
gently contoured shape and high-gloss colours have
put it in many high-design nursery collections. There
are two modes: Standard, 8 hours at 300ml/hr; or
Long Run Mode, 18 hours at 130ml/hr. The humidifier
is 15.2 cm (6 in.) high and 30.5 cm (12 in.) in
diameter. It comes in six colours: bright orange, pale
pink, pale blue, white, cream and black.

MobiCam Ultra

Mobi, USA
www.getmobi.com

The young creatives who brought us the TykeLight
Buddy (see p. 236) are pioneers also in the world of
baby monitors. With the MobiCam Ultra they offer a
camera with tiltable eye and 4.6 cm (1¾ in.) monitor
screen with high-resolution TFT colour. The video
camera has a 91 m (300 ft) range (night vision up to
3.6 m/12 ft). Both units are compact and the system
can be augmented with two additional cameras. Mobi
have also launched a digital wireless audio monitor
in streamlined, hand-moulded design.

Accessories

Bath, Storage

New parents are often amazed by the amount of kit one
small baby can require or at least inspire their carers
to believe that they need. From buggies, to highchairs
to bassinets and bouncers, the really bulky items are
the ones that seem to add up in the early days and keep
mothers, fathers and grandparents racing around the
nearest shopping centre or the internet to compare
componentry, safety features and ease of use alongside
a host of other design elements. And then there are other
things that are not absolutely necessary, but useful, and
those things that are useful and also a little bit of a
luxury. Many of the products presented in this book fall
into the latter category due to the degree of design and
gadgetry attached to them.

However, when we talk about accessories we are necessarily
implying 'extras'. But sometimes the extras make a big
difference in the way the basics are carried out or how
much work or fun we have doing them. Following are some
pleasantly surprising solutions for bathing, changing, storing
and protecting that are all a little bit whimsical, but at
least offer the possibility of making the everyday chores
of parenting a bit more palatable and in some cases even
what you might describe as fun. Some are just delightful
bits of design and are worth admiring just for that reason.

Fish Bath Thermometer

NScessity, UK
www.nscessity.co.uk

It is a green fish that reads out the temperature of the bath water while it floats around the bath tub – and when it is not being picked up and bitten or battered by the little bather. There are many bath thermometers on the market, but this adds a pleasing character design that is also modern, colourful and not overly garish. The shape is easy to grip and it is just a joy to look at and use. It is also a serious health aid, since thousands of children are scalded every year by hot water.

Jellybaby Changing Mat, Bath Toy Store

Steve Küster
Küster, UK
www.kuster.co.uk

Following on from the success of his highchairs (see p. 77), designer Steve Küster developed a line of children's furnishings and accessories. The Jellybaby changing mat is a real innovation and improvement on the vinyl-covered foam mats of old. Made of ergonomically shaped memory foam, it is washable, hygienic and durable and will not crack or fade. It also comes with a washable terry cover. The Bath Toy Store is also a very logical invention; the brightly coloured, but nicely styled, bins have holes in the bottom to drain water out while the toys are stacked neatly inside.

Potty Bench

Rebecca Finell
Boon, USA
www.booninc.com

Designer Rebecca Finell was on a roll after the Flair
highchair (see p. 74). With the Frog Pod (below)
and the Potty Bench she is a one-woman campaign
to tidy up the bathroom. The Potty Bench is a
multifunctioning little unit that is a seat for parents
while bathing their child (supports up to 136 kg/300
lb), a step stool for children and a training potty with
clever removable drawer, two side compartments
for wipes and other supplies, and a toilet roll holder.

Frog Pod

Rebecca Finell
Boon, USA
www.booninc.com

This is not an object for parents who want to make
statements about high design, but rather those who
are interested in things that are designed well so that
children like them and parents find them useful. In
a home with small children, where the bath tub can
start to look like a toy box, wall-mounted toy caddies
have become a near necessity. Designer Rebecca
Finell (see above) created the Frog Pod, which
improves on the popular suction-attached net caddy
in a number of ways. First, unlike suction devices,
which invariably slide at some point down into the
bath, the Frog Pod attaches semi-permanently to any
bath tub wall using adhesive strips, which can later
be removed. It can also be screw-mounted to other
surfaces. It features a top shelf to hold products such
as shampoo and bubble bath. The main body is a 'toy
scoop', which can be removed and replaced easily and
also allows for drainage, and the frog 'fingers and
toes' can be used to hang scrubbers or cloths.

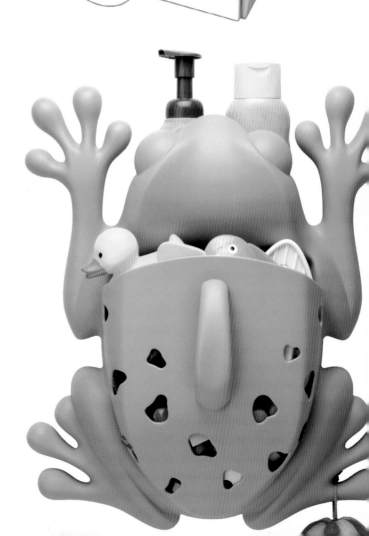

Pet Shirts

Rosario Hurtado, Roberto Feo
El Ultimo Grito, UK
www.elultimogrito.co.uk

The wild world of El Ultimo Grito (see also pp. 109, 122) is one where anthropomorphism rules. Their creative crossovers include these surprising stuffed-animal storage sacks. Cloth bags shaped as dogs or cars 'come to life' as the designers say, 'when they are filled with all those things that we no longer use, but which we do not want to part with.' They can also be filled with the assorted clothing, soft toys and any other articles that would otherwise end up being strewn over the floor.

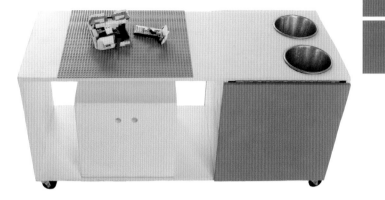

Noah Building Table, Owyn Toy Box

Kiersten Hathcock
Modmom, USA
www.modmomfurniture.com

Inspired by her son's love of making Lego constructions and leaving them all around the house, self-taught furniture designer Kiersten Hathcock went to her garage workshop and came up with this rolling table made from birch ply, which can be stored with Lego creations stuck firmly to its top display board. Two inset canisters hold a supply of bricks, and a swing-up cabinet door conceals storage, while a square seat fits on the shelf underneath. The Owyn Toy Box brings a bit of beauty to kids' storage with two compartments fitted with coloured leaf lids and inlaid branch pattern.

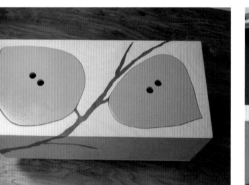

Fuji Toy Box

Jenny Argie, Andrew Thornton
Argington, USA
www.argington.com

This is another work of wondrous woodcraft from Jenny Argie and Andrew Thornton at Argington (see pp. 95, 98, 114). The Fuji Toy Box is a basic wooden box with sturdy locking hinges that are also slow closing for safety, and a useful little display shelf set within the base. Made from sustainable hard wood, it is available in a range of woodstain finishes and with coloured seat cushions.

Box 1

Nume, Italy
www.nume-design.it

The designers at Nume have created a world of well-crafted furnishings and accessories for children using mostly natural materials in shapes and hues that are simple and subtle without being bland. This baby ring is a one of the most basic of tools, and offers a little respite to the carer of a rolling or early crawling baby. The removable cotton cover comes in a choice of colours.

Clothes Tree

P'kolino, USA
www.pkolino.com

P'kolino's 'playfully smart' aesthetic extends to helping children keep organized and tidy. The Clothes Tree is a wonderfully sculptural coloured structure made of sturdy Baltic birch and painted in water-based white, orange or green, or left in natural wood hue. A wide base and solid, single-form construction (no nuts, bolts or pegs) make it stable and durable.

Pop Bin

Johanna Leestma LaFleur
Loom, Inc, USA
www.loomlife.com

Since starting up her own design company in 2003, Johanna Leestma LaFleur has applied her skill with fabric and pattern to a number of bags and carriers (see p. 206) and has gone on to make other objects that are a pleasure to use and to look at. Pop Bins are made from smooth, durable 100 per cent cotton canvas (soon to be available in nylon) stretched on an expanding metal frame. There are bright-patterned details, and the bins are made in two sizes.

Hanger 1

Nume, Italy
www.nume-design.it

Like most of the products in the Nume catalogue, these hanging pegs are very basic and yet somehow very appealing. They are made of natural birch ply and have coloured knobs.

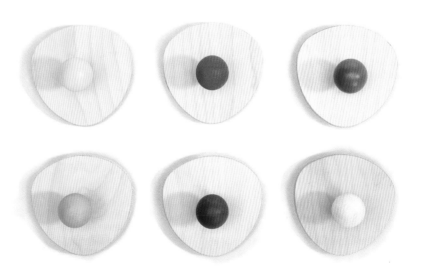

Albert Wall Hanger,
Ape Hanger

Christopher Robin Nordström
Our Children's Gorilla, Sweden
www.ourchildrensgorilla.com

Designer Christopher Robin Nordström created his Albert Wall Hanger as a tribute to his own passion for 1980s space toys. For these and the Ape Hanger, his driving idea was that 'If you want to encourage kids to do something, you do it best by making it fun.' Albert is made in metal; Ape Hanger is in valchromat fibreboard. (See also pp. 129, 192, 194.)

Kiddy Guard

Lascal, Sweden
www.lascal.se

This improvement on the stairgate comes from the same Swedish geniuses who brought us the Buggyboard (see p. 32). The Kiddy Guard operates like a roller blind, so it rolls up neatly to the side when not in use. There is a toddler-proof lock, which can be operated by adults using one hand (when the other is holding the baby). Made of wipe-clean material that can withstand an impact of up to 100 kg (220 lb), the Kiddy Guard can fit an opening up to 130 cm (51 in.) wide.

Universal Buggy Cover

Margaret de Haas
Koeka, Netherlands
www.koeka.nl

With the rise of premium-priced buggies on the market, designer Margaret de Haas offers parents an opportunity to change or renew their buggy seat without great expense. Koeka's Universal Buggy Cover is made of the same high-quality soft terry towelling as their blankets and mats (see p. 158), but is designed to fit the most recent buggy chassis or car seat. It comes in a range of bright colours.

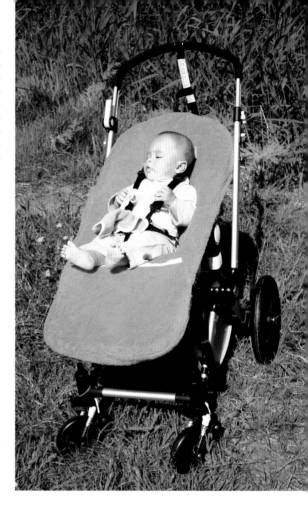

Animal Bag

Rebecca Finell
Boon, USA
www.booninc.com

Most parents have particular difficulty getting rid of their children's stuffed toys either for reasons of sentimental attachment or because they have become too well loved to survive another child. Either way they do seem to mount up and Rebecca Finell and Boon (see also p. 243) have offered a solution in a faux-fur zippered bag that makes a soft seat out of piles of soft toys. The washable cover has mesh windows that let you see what is inside. The bag is available in three shapes/sizes.

Shakeaway Latte

phil&teds, New Zealand
www.philandteds.com

It seems the designers at phil&teds might just succeed in making parenting more of the kind of adventure people might aspire to, as their range of gear looks more and more like that of experienced outward-bound explorers. Where a rock-climber might pack energy drinks, the travelling parent now has the Shakeaway Latte, a specially designed feed bottle that holds premeasured formula powder in the cap and sterilized water in the vessel. When ready to feed, you twist the cap to release the powder into the water and 'shake away'. Like most specialist gear designers, phil&teds have created a special cover and bag for the whole system.

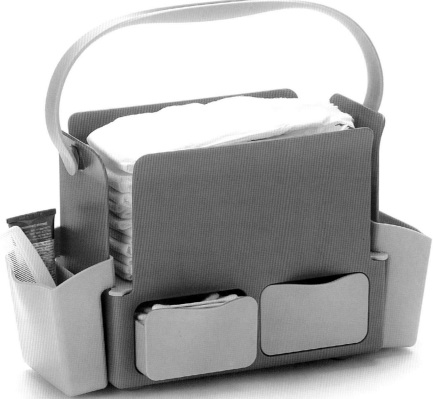

Toolbox

Scott Henderson
SKIP*HOP, USA
www.skiphop.com

Especially in the early days, routine baby changing and cleaning can require quite a few extra items and it is not always very convenient to have them stored in one place. The Toolbox is a portable, washable changing station with a main compartment for up to a dozen nappies, or diapers, removable side pockets for creams and wipes and drawers for cotton buds or other necessities.

Designed for Kids
Acknowledgments

Special thanks to Jane Aresti for additional picture and product research. Thanks also to Jonathan Haycock at Funktionalley for help with several Scandinavian products; Marion Kern at Rasselfisch for help locating designers of products on their fantasic site; Claire Fife at Dangling Carrot for help with Trunki, Razor, Didicar and other great toys; Andy Fensom for information on phil&teds; Katherina Marginter at das Moebel for introducing me to some wonderful Austrian designers; Ali Records at Velocity Art and Design and Mark Eldsness at Sparkability for giving access to their well-edited collections; Danni Lindley at Dorel; Barry Nicholson at Offi; Helga Ekdahl at Brio; Sandra Heinisch at HABA; Cristina Fava and Alberto Ferrari at BRAVO Communicazione for Aprica; MaryAnn Poole at Micro Scooters, UK; and the dozens of people who returned endless email queries and sent and re-sent images for the book. I also owe a debt to the writers/product reporters at www.babygadget.net for highlighting new and wonderful products.

Thank you to Paola Antonelli, Yves Béhar, Tom Dixon, Greg Lynn, John Maeda and Scott Wilson for giving their time and comments.

To Lucas Dietrich for inspiring the book, Cat Glover for making sure everything was in the right place at the right time, and to Peter Dawson and Tegan Danko at Grade for their design genius, as always. And, for Mom.

The following websites are among the best for promoting new and innovative design:
www.modernseed.com furnishings, toys and accessories
www.sparkability.com furnishings, toys and accessories with many European designs
www.babygeared.com high-design furnishings and accessories
www.babygadget.net continually updated blog/product review
www.velocityartanddesign.com high-design and innovative products
www.bibsandstuff.com UK distributor for good European and US brands
www.bumpsmaternity.com UK distributor for some better brands and designs
www.funkymoose.co.uk UK source for good European and US brands
www.interinnovationsuk.com (for Strolli Rider in the UK)
www.babylonia.be hammocks and hanging beds
www.rasselfisch.com toys and accessories
www.dasmoebel.at independent design furniture
www.tinydodo.com toys and accessories
www.poaa.com objects by designers
www.moederflets.nl (bicycles and seats)
www.funktionalley.com Scandinavian design toys and accessories

First published in 2008 in hardcover in the United States of America by Thames & Hudson Inc., 500 Fifth Avenue, New York, New York 10110
thamesandhudsonusa.com

Library of Congress Catalog Card Number 2008900997

ISBN 978-0-500-51413-9

Book design and layout:
Grade Design Consultants, London

Printed and bound in China by C&C Offset Printing Co Ltd.

Picture Credits

C = cover; T = top; A = above; M = middle; B = below; L = left; R = right

9, 21 Bugaboo; C, 10, 16T, 83, 170, 217B Aprica; C, 11, 15T HTS, Norway; 12T, 19, 60T Orbit; C, 12B Takata, Japan; 13, 14, 15B, 16B, 22, 213B Dorel; 17, 24, 25, 61T, 72, 204B Mutsy; C, 18T, 39, 62B, 70 bloom; 18B Mountain Buggy; C, 20, 74L, 52B, 178 Brio; C, 3, 23 Stokke; 26 WIP, srl; 27 BOB Trailers; 28L 3playing; C, 2, 28R, 29, 61B, 211T, 216, 223T, 225B, 251T phil&teds; 30 Worrell Inc; 31T Buggypod; 3, 31B, 34 Chariot Carriers; 32, 206, 229B, 249 Cheeky Rascals, UK; 33 Lamprecht; 35T, 186B islabikes; 35B Chung; 36T Nihola; 36B Gazelle; 37, 91 Funktionalley; C, 40-41 Messier Designers; C, 42T, 164B E27; 42B, 43T, 59B, 99T, 169 Nurseryworks; 43B Studio Zero Aarnio; 44T Babylonia; 44B, 120B Green Lullaby; 45 Knoppa; 46R photo Keld Pedersen; 47T Monte Design Group; 47B Moffi Ltd; 48, 127 Chul Min Kang, industREALdesign; C, 49T, 79 Selmi; C, 2, 49B, 112T, 120T; 121; 127B; 129T courtesy of Offi and Company; 50 portrait, photo Mike McGregor; 52T, 58, 71, 96, 119 ducduc; 53 photo Keld Pedersen; C, 2, 54-5, 75 Stokke; 56 Ooba; C, 57 Netto Collection; C, 59T, 97 Oeuf; 60B Bumbo; 62T, 222T Delta Diffusion; 63 Mohr Polster; C, 64 Svan; 65 BabyBjörn; 67, 90T, 100, 141B, 165 photo Julie Toy, courtesy notNeutral; 68 photo Per Sørensen; 69 AGEDesign; C, 3, 73 Mozzee; 74R, 243, 250B Boon; 76, 174T fuseproject; 77T, 242B Küster; 77B, 115B Sasaki Design International; 78 Studio Maartje Steenkamp/Inga Powillett; 82 Alfredo Häberli/Littala; 83B © WMF AG; C, 84, 202, 251B Skip*Hop; 85T, 139, 154T Absolute Zero Degrees; 85B, 128T Richard Hutten Studio; C, 86 French Bull; 87 Stelton A/S; 88 Rivadossi Sandro; C, 2, 3, 89, 94T, 112B, 113T, 156, 246T, 247B Nume, Italy; C, 93, 111 Bobles; 94B, 248T,M Modmom; 95T, 106T, 196B, 199T, 235 Habitat, UK; C, 3, 95B, 98, 114, 245B Argington; 99B Warber; 101 sixeight; 102-3 Eric Pfeiffer/courtesy of Offi and Company; 104T Monica Castiglioni; 104AM © Patrick Gries; C, 1-2, 106B, 110, 164T, 191 Magis; 107T Basander Lundin; 107B photo Exit Studio; C, 108, 246B P'kolino; 109, 122, 241, 244 El Ultimo Grito; 113B Jennifer Delonge; 115 Collect Furniture; C, 116-7 photo Marc Eggimann, © Vitra www.vitra.com, courtesy Vitra and Herman Miller, USA; 118T Thomas Maitz, Periudi; C, 118B, 126B Lisa Albin, Iglooplay; 119T Thorsten van Elten; 123 photo Marc-Pierre Morel; 124 Daniel Kron/GeniusJones; 125T Alfredo Häberli, Offect; 125B Fatboy; 126T Dieter Paul, Dmp; C, 128B, 197B, 205B RoomMate; 129B, 192B, 248 Our Children's Gorilla; 130, 193 images by Antonio Marconi, supplied by art directors ZPZ Partners, © Play+; C, 131 Louise Campbell/Erik Jørgensen; 133, 151 Gustav Maxwell & Co; 134 Flensted; 135 Oras Designs; 136, 140 Wee Gallery; 137, 161R Vilac; 138 Inke Heiland/Inke; 141 Jenny Wilkinson Studio; 142 WallCandy Arts; 143T Magscapes; 143B StickyUps; 144L, 152 Sandberg; 145 e-glue; 146T portrait Hainsley Brown; 148 Pixel; 149T Anja Grabenhorst/Apple Pie; 149B Dwell; 150L Lotus Linens; 150R Denyse Schmidt Quilts; 153 Hans-Jörgen Hansson/Egget Design; 155, 197T Pia Eriksson Textilverkstad; 157 Boodalee; 158, 250T Koeka; 160-61 Nani Marquina; 162L Lili Latifi; 162-3 Boym; C, 164B, 174B, 231 HABA; 166-7 The Rug Company, UK; C, 3, 169, 172-3 Alex Hochstrasser/Active People; 171T Manhattan Toy Company; C, 171B, 177B, 184B Zolo; 175L Fat Brain Toy Co.; 175R Scott Klinker/courtesy of Offi & Company; 176T Cuboro; 176B Geomag SA; 177T Lego; 179 Automoblox; C, 3, 180-81L photo Jonas Lindström; 182 Kukua; 183 Didicar; 184T Ineke Hans; 185, 194B Helemill, UK; 186T Razor; C, 187 Micro Mobility; 190, 195T Kidsonroof; 192T Chad Holder; 195B Nico Schweizer/Momoll; 196T Pook!; 198T Pusefix; 198B Treasure Trove Toys; 199B Pixel Blocks; C, 201, 207 Trunki; 203 Fleurville; 204T Jack Spade; 205, 247T Loom; 208T Samsonite, UK; C, 208B, 219T Deuter; 209T Little Lifestyles; 209B CBH Studio; 210 Lillébaby; 211B Hippychick; 212 Matali Crasset/Pinpon; C, 214, 220-21 Weybury Hildreth; 215, 224 BabyBjörn; 217R, 222B Nomad; 218T, 223B Macpac; 219B Bushbaby; 225 Kaboost, USA; 227, 229T Vessel Inc; 228 J Schatz; C, 230, 242T NCessity; 234 Glide Inc.; 236T, 239B Mobi, USA; 236B Karl Merkl/Merkled; 237T Babytec International Products Ltd; C, 237B courtesy of www.mathmos.com; 238T Grobag, UK; C, 238B Philips, Netherlands; 239T Plusminuszero, Japan/www.dynamism.com